Guiding Your Parish Through the Christian Initiation Process:

A Handbook for Leaders

Guiding Your Parish Through the Christian Initiation Process:

A Handbook for Leaders

William R. Bruns

St.
Anthony
Messenger
Press

CINCINNATI, OHIO

Nihil Obstat: Rev. Lawrence Landini, O.F.M.
Rev. Robert Hagedorn

Imprimi Potest: Rev. John Bok, O.F.M.
Provincial

Imprimatur: Rev. R. Daniel Conlon, Vicar General
Archdiocese of Cincinnati
February 1, 1993

The *nihil obstat* and *imprimatur* are a declaration that a book is considered to be free from doctrinal or moral error. It is not implied that those who have granted the *nihil obstat* and *imprimatur* agree with the contents, opinions or statements expressed.

Scripture citations are taken from *The New American Bible With Revised New Testament*, copyright ©1986 by the Confraternity of Christian Doctrine, and are used by permission. All rights reserved. Excerpts from the English translation of *Lectionary for Mass*, copyright ©1969, International Committee on English in the Liturgy, Inc. (ICEL); excerpts from the English translation of *The Roman Missal*, copyright ©1973, ICEL; excerpts from the English translation of *Rite of Christian Initiation of Adults*, copyright ©1985, ICEL. All rights reserved. Excerpts taken from *Rite of Christian Initiation of Adults*, copyright ©1988 by the United States Catholic Conference, 3211 Fourth Street, N.E., Washington, D.C. 20017-1194, are used with permission. All rights reserved. For a copy of this publication, please call 1-800-235-USCC(8722) and ask for publication number 213-6. The excerpts from *The Documents of Vatican II*, edited by Austin P. Flannery, copyright ©1988 by Costello Publishing Co., Inc., are reprinted with permision of Costello Publishing Co., Inc., Northport, New York.

Cover and book design by Julie Lonneman

ISBN 0-86716-188-4

Published by St. Anthony Messenger Press
Printed in the U.S.A.

Dedicated to

The Most Reverend Edward T. O'Meara, S.T.D.

1921-1992

Archbishop of Indianapolis
1980-1992

A singularly gracious man

whose openness and expansiveness of spirit

gave us a glimpse of the face of Jesus.

May he rest in peace.

Acknowledgments

No book is ever published without the help and involvement of many, many people. Their contributions cannot go unacknowledged, nor can my sincere appreciation go unspoken:

• To the Reverend Paul M. Shikany, J.C.L., vice vicar judicial of the Metropolitan Tribunal of the Archdiocese of Indianapolis, who patiently guided me through the intricacies of canon law—always with a profound sensitivity to the pastoral questions.

• To Alexa Suelzer, S.P., Ph.D., professor of theology and philosophy, Saint Mary-of-the-Woods College, who was kind enough to read the complete manuscript of this book and provide numerous helpful comments and suggestions. Words of thanks also go to Sr. Alexa and her sister, Sister Mary Josephine Suelzer, S.P., Ph.D., for helping to elucidate some of the finer points of Latin grammar that are not as clear to me now as they might have been thirty years ago.

• To all those team members, inquirers, catechumens and candidates who have shared the journey with me over the years, especially

> Karen Oddi, a model director of the Order of Initiation

> Rose Kavanaugh, who knows no strangers and who knows just how to walk the journey as an abiding companion

> Joan Frame, S.P., Kathleen Murnane, Sallie Bruns and Blanche Stewart, ministers of initiation at the Cathedral Church of Saints Peter and Paul, in Indianapolis

> The Reverend John N. Sciarra, now "retired" and my pastor for nearly twenty-five years, who quickly recognized the efficacy and importance of the Order of Initiation and whose early enthusiasm and celebration of the various rites helped entice me into this ministry.

Contents

Introduction

This book is written primarily for my sisters and brothers in the Catholic Church who have just begun to minister in the initiation process through which new Christians are made[1] and through which they are brought into the Catholic Christian community.

It may help readers to know a few things right away: I have walked in your shoes. Since the early 1980's, I have had the distinct good fortune to be involved in the Order of Christian Initiation of Adults. When my pastor asked me if I would be "interested" in serving on the parish's RCIA team, I said, "Yes!" And at my first meeting, I found that I had been named director of the catechumenate! Not a unique story, I'm sure.

This book is meant to be a basic "starter kit." It makes no assumptions regarding your knowledge of, or experience with, the *Rite of Christian Initiation of Adults*. In fact, if you are one of the many who have stepped forward into this ministry with little or no knowledge of what you were committing yourself to, but with a firm conviction about your call to this ministry, then this book is written especially for you. I can only assume that you have agreed (as I did many years ago) to undertake this ministry while "under the influence"...the influence of the Holy Spirit!

It is my hope that this book will provide you with down-to-earth information—grounded in good theological principles and tempered in the furnace of pastoral practice. It is also my hope that this information will enable you to grow in the ministry you have undertaken and, in truth, to fulfill the plan and purposes of the Holy Spirit for your involvement in this most challenging and graced work of the Church.

Praised be Jesus Christ!

William R. Bruns
Memorial of Augustine of Hippo
1992

1

1. Preliminary Questions

Q. What is the Rite of Christian Initiation of Adults?

A. The Rite of Christian Initiation of Adults is the way people are now initiated into the Christian way of life, specifically in the Roman Catholic tradition. Through it, the Church in the twentieth century has restored the ancient catechumenate, which existed in its fullest form between the second and the fifth centuries of the Christian era.

This restoration was officially called for on December 4, 1963, when the Second Vatican Council promulgated the *Constitution on the Sacred Liturgy (Sacrosanctum concilium)*, the first document approved by the council. In that document, the council fathers mandated the reestablishment of the catechumenate with these two rather simple and forthright sentences:

> The catechumenate for adults, comprising several distinct steps, is to be restored and brought into use at the discretion of the local ordinary. By this means the time of the catechumenate, which is intended as a period of suitable instruction, may be sanctified by sacred rites to be celebrated at successive intervals of time.
> (*Constitution on the Sacred Liturgy*, 64)

Provisional rites were distributed in 1966; a second draft of the rites was distributed for experimental use in 1969. But it was not until January 6, 1972, in the document *Ordo initiationis christianae adultorum*, that the rites were promulgated for general use. However, the official English translation of that 1972 document, the *Rite of Christian Initiation of Adults*, did not appear until 1974.

In 1986, the bishops of the United States approved adaptations to the rite, and they also approved thirty-seven national statutes (rules and options for the rite peculiar to the United States). The Vatican confirmed the adaptations in February 1987; implementation of the Order of Initiation, with its U.S. adaptations and the national statutes, became mandatory in the United States

3

on September 1, 1988.

Q. I always hear this program referred to as the RCIA. What do the letters *RCIA* stand for?

A. The initials *RCIA* stand for *R*ite of *C*hristian *I*nitiation of *A*dults. This is the English translation of the title of the official Church document, in Latin *Ordo initiationis christianae adultorum.*

People in particular fields often develop and use specialized vocabularies to make communication faster and more specific. One example of this is the use of acronyms and initializations (for example, RADAR for Radio Detecting and Ranging; EPA for Environmental Protection Agency). *RCIA* is one such initialization in Church circles.

One reason a special language has grown up around Church ministry, including that of the Rite of Christian Initiation of Adults, is that many terms and concepts that have come to us from ancient Church traditions do not translate easily into twentieth-century English.

In this book, while I'll need to use this special language, I'll do my best to explain strange words and expressions as I go along. If you come across a word that isn't explained in the text, check the Glossary (see page 132).

For all its merits, the use of specialized language has several serious drawbacks. We can become so used to the abbreviated versions of things that we forget not only what the abbreviations stand for, but also what the core concepts are. Abbreviated ways of speaking and writing can eventually lead to abbreviated thinking and to truncated concepts.

In addition, while technical language functions to include those who "speak the language," it has the indirect effect of excluding those who do not. The last thing I want to do is exclude anyone. So, in addition to explaining any unfamiliar terms, I will also follow the policy of not using the initialization *RCIA* as a noun. This is the policy adopted by *Church* magazine and by the North American Forum on the Catechumenate, the leading group in the United States devoted to the effective implementation of the Rite of Christian Initiation of Adults.

4

In this book, then, the Rite of Christian Initiation of Adults will be referred to as the *process*, *rite*, *rite of initiation*, *rite of Christian initiation*, *Ordo* (when referring to the document itself), *Order*, *Order of Initiation*, and so forth.

Q. Why "Order"? And what do you mean by *Ordo*?

A. Church documents that set forth the rituals for the celebration of the sacraments and rites have titles that usually begin with the Latin word *ordo*, which means an *order* or *arrangement*. The root meaning of this Latin word has to do with weaving and with the row of threads on a loom. Hence, *ordo* suggests an orderly weaving together of separate things into whole cloth.

In the Church documents we are talking about, the word is used for the order of the service. For instance, the Latin title for the ceremony for the celebration of the Mass is *Ordo Missae* (the *Order of the Mass*); the ritual for the sacrament of the sick is called in Latin *Ordo unctionis infirmorum eorumque pastoralis curae* (literally, the *Order of the Anointing of the Sick and of Their Pastoral Care*), known officially in English as *Pastoral Care of the Sick: Rites of Anointing and Viaticum*.

Q. But why the change now? I've heard this process referred to as "the RCIA" for many years now.

A. Almost from the very beginning, in the 1970's, folks involved with the *Rite of Christian Initiation of Adults* have been trying to characterize it—trying to capture its essence—in one or two words. Apparently, this has not been easy to do, because the discussion continues.

In the very early days, many people thought of and talked about the rite as a "program." But programs have definite beginnings and endings; the Rite of Christian Initiation of Adults has neither. In addition, the rite is not a religious education program. It is not essentially about information; it is about conversion.

When the term *program* was discarded, the word (and concept) *process* replaced it. Unlike a program, a process does not come in blocks of time determined by its creators and implementors; the length of a process is determined by the individuals for whom it was designed.

The process involved in the Rite of Christian Initiation of Adults is (or should be) determined by the individuals for whom it is meant; that is, each individual moves along at her or his own pace, with the leaders, or facilitators, responding to each individual's pace and needs, not vice versa. In this regard, the Rite of Christian Initiation of Adults is a process.

Just about the time most people began getting comfortable with the concept of the Rite of Christian Initiation of Adults as a process, Aidan Kavanagh, O.S.B., a monk of Saint Meinrad Archabbey and professor of liturgics and dean of Yale Divinity School, suggested that the essential identity of the Rite of Christian Initiation of Adults is precisely that of *rite*. It is, after all, a sacrament, or rather a grouping of sacraments—Baptism, Confirmation, Eucharist. According to Kavanagh's understanding, it is essentially a sacramental rite.

A few more years went by, years of thinking about and working with the rite of initiation. Recently, others have suggested that it would be more correct to refer to the rite as an Order. They believe that translating *Ordo* in the Latin title of the document as *Rite* is not really a good choice. In addition, calling it a rite gives too much emphasis to its public liturgical aspects, often to the detriment of its other components. Translating *Ordo* as *Rite* also ignores the fact that the entire process comprises many individual rites that, in turn, make up three sacraments. It may be best, then, to call the Rite of Christian Initiation of Adults an *Order*. This is a more faithful translation of the original Latin title of the document. And as we have seen, it also suggests the weaving together of all the different aspects of the process.

Q. How does the Order of Initiation differ from inquiry classes?

A. The differences are significant. Perhaps the image of a traditional classroom best captures the differences. In the front of the room is the teacher who imparts knowledge to the students, all of whom are seated in straight rows of desks, neatly lined up one behind the other.

Now, imagine the same room with all the desks removed. In their places are comfortable chairs arranged in a circle. Look around for the "teacher." Where is she? Where is he? In a meeting of inquirers or catechumens, the leader will be found seated in the circle among the inquirers or catechumens, team members, priest and others. These contrasting images give you a sense of the differences in approach that the Order of Initiation envisions.

Classes involve teachers and students. The Order of Initiation involves a group of learners who fulfill a variety of roles: the local community, facilitators, the bishop, sponsors, catechumens, priests, deacons, companions, inquirers, catechists and others. *All* are learners.

When we speak of inquiry classes, the term *classes* indicates an educational model and implies that religious education is the primary concern. The Order of Initiation, on the other hand, speaks of conversion and community, of hospitality and welcoming, of formation and of the sharing of faith as well as the sharing of lives.

The term *classes* speaks of programs; the Order envisions a process. Programs are usually designed with a beginning point and an ending point (some ending points may even feature a "graduation" of some sort).

Programs are set up and people fit themselves into the program boundaries. For instance, you might see something like this in a Sunday bulletin:

> The Social Action Committee of St. Richard Parish is sponsoring a series of programs on the Wednesday evenings of Lent from 7:30 to 9:00 p.m. in the school cafeteria. This year's topic: "From *Rerum Novarum* to *Centesimus Annus*: One Hundred Years of Catholic Social Teaching." There is no admission charge.

In this example, you have a program with boundaries:

- A beginning: the first Wednesday of Lent.
- An ending: the Wednesday of Holy Week.
- Time slots: 7:30 p.m. until 9:00 p.m.
- Set topic: the social encyclicals.

This adult education program, precisely because it is a *program*, has been arranged for (what the committee hopes will be) the

7

convenience and interests of as many members of St. Richard Parish as possible. However, if some members of the parish have other commitments on Wednesday evenings or can only be present for the first and last sessions, they must just pass up all or most of this great program. In addition, all that the program designers will be able to say about the social teaching of the Church must be fitted into the agreed-upon time slots.

A process, however, begins with the participants themselves who, to a great extent, determine the agenda, the length of time that they will participate based on their individual needs and, in some instances, even the time and the day of gathering. (Can't make it on Wednesday evenings? How about Friday mornings?)

The Order of Initiation is not just another program. It is at the heart of what the Church is about: proclaiming the Good News of Jesus Christ to all who will listen and calling the entire world to initial and continual conversion—a turning away from That-Which-Is-Not-God and a turning toward the One-Who-Is, the One we call God. This conversion may take place through a first-time relationship with Jesus Christ and his community of believers or through a deepened relationship with the one whom we proclaim as Messiah and Lord.

In the Order of Initiation, there really are no experts—and there certainly are no "outside experts." All involved in the Order are on a journey together; no one is an outsider. And the journey is one of continual conversion. Oh, one hopes that those facilitating the sessions are "expert" at group dynamics, on the ins and outs of the rite, on faith sharing and so forth. But no one—not even the pastor—is an expert in the sense that she or he "has arrived" or has the whole "Truth" that just needs to be handed on to the inquirers. All are on a journey; all have a piece of the truth that they are willing to share.

These are the major differences between the vision of the Order of Initiation and inquiry classes. The Order of Initiation is not neat, predictable or tidy because to be at its most effective, it must meet people where they are. As James B. Dunning, president of the North American Forum on the Catechumenate, is so fond of pointing out, "It's a messy, messy thing that we've gotten ourselves into. But life itself is messy, so why should we expect anything different in our faith life?"

2. Ministries

Q. What are the various roles and ministries involved in the Order of Initiation?

A. The Order seeks to involve the entire community. But within the community, a variety of roles and ministries exist. The *Ordo* itself calls for several specific ministries; pastoral needs and practice have brought forth others.

Here are the ministers and ministries called for by the *Ordo*:

The Community. The initiation of new members can only take place within the context of a community of believers.[2]

"[T]he initiation of adults is the responsibility of all the baptized.... Hence, the entire community must help the candidates and the catechumens throughout the process of initiation..." (*RCIA*, 9). Gone are the days when joining the Church was a private or semiprivate affair between the priest who gave instructions to the convert and then baptized that individual in a nearly empty church on a Sunday afternoon in the presence of only the convert's godparent(s), family and friends.

Sponsor. The sponsor is a person who knows the candidate well, who accompanies the candidate on the faith journey, and who testifies publicly in liturgical ceremonies to the candidate's moral character, faith and intention—that is, to the candidate's readiness to advance to each new step in the process. A sponsor may also be the candidate's godparent, but that is not necessarily so (*RCIA*, 10).

Godparent. An individual's godparent establishes a spiritual relationship with the candidate that lasts forever. In the year that the candidate will be baptized, the godparent journeys with him or her usually from the First Sunday of Lent through the entire Lenten season to the Easter Vigil and initiation by Baptism, Confirmation and Eucharist, then continues through mystagogy (the postbaptismal period) and into eternity.

A godparent upholds the candidate in times of fear or hesitation, testifies to the candidate's readiness, serves as a model and guides the candidate in the Christian life. The godparent, chosen by the candidate, must be a fully initiated Catholic, that is, a Catholic who has been baptized and confirmed and who has received the Eucharist. The godparent is delegated by the parish and approved by the priest (*RCIA*, 11).

(For more discussion about godparents, see "Pastoral Situations," page 91.)

Catechist. The catechist has the responsibility of presenting the faith to the candidates and of being visibly and actively involved in the liturgical rites. Catechists may, when authorized by the bishop, perform minor exorcisms and give blessings. A competent catechist is more than a "religion teacher"; a competent catechist's ministry and life must "echo," or resound with, the Good News of Jesus Christ (*RCIA*, 16).

Bishop. The bishop of the diocese is responsible for establishing, regulating and promoting the initiation process in his particular Church (the diocesan Church), and, at the Rite of Election, he admits candidates to the next celebration of the Easter sacraments (*RCIA*, 12).

(After catechumens are chosen [elected] by God and the Church at the Rite of Election to celebrate the initiation sacraments at the next Easter Vigil, they are called the *elect*.)

Priest. The priest presides at the celebration of the initiation sacraments and oversees the celebration of all the rites of the Order of Initiation. He also has pastoral care of the candidates and may work with the deacon and catechists in providing catechesis. The priest approves the candidate's selection of a godparent (*RCIA*, 13, 14).

Deacon. Throughout the entire process, the deacon assists in a variety of ways, including catechesis. The needs of individual communities will determine the specific role of the deacon (*RCIA*, 15).

Here are some ministers and ministries that are not specifically called for by the *Ordo* but that have developed in response to pastoral needs:

Coordinator/Director of the Order of Initiation. This individual has overall coordinating responsibility in a local faith community for the entire Order of Christian Initiation of Adults. While the *Ordo* calls on the bishop to exercise overall direction of the initiation process for the entire diocese, the local, day-to-day responsibilities in each parish are delegated to others.

The size of modern dioceses, at least in the United States and Canada, makes the bishop's personal involvement in the Order of Initiation at the parish level a virtual impossibility. My diocese, the Archdiocese of Indianapolis, comprises some 200,000 members living in 39 counties (approximately 13,500 square miles) and worshiping in about 160 local communities or parishes.

Over the years, pastoral need has required the appointment of a director, or coordinator, of the Order of Initiation at the parish level. Some parishes call this person the director of the catechumenate, but this title is something of a technical misnomer, since (as we shall see later) the catechumenate is only one of several periods involved in the entire Order of Initiation.

Companion. A companion may accompany a particular candidate or may be present for, and available to, the entire group during the journey of faith. While everyone involved in the Order of Initiation may be said to carry out this ministry, often a particular parishioner is uniquely gifted to fulfill this companioning in a special, focused way. The most effective companions are those people who are open, warm, friendly, easy to talk to and be with, and knowledgeable about the local faith community (perhaps long-time members of the parish).

Liturgist. The liturgist has responsibilities for overseeing and adapting the implementation of the various liturgical rites of the *Ordo*. (See "Liturgical Rites," page 43.) If the liturgist for the rites of initiation is a different person from the parish's liturgy director or coordinator, then the Order's liturgist must work closely with those involved in the parish's general liturgical celebrations.

Liturgical Musician. The liturgical musician is responsible for the choice and execution of the music used during the liturgical rites. If the liturgical musician for the Order is a different person from the parish's director of liturgical music, then, once again, close collaboration among all those involved is essential.

Mystagogue. The mystagogue is a catechist with a special focus: the direction of catechesis for the newly baptized (called *neophytes,* that is *new plants, seedlings*) during the year following their baptisms.

Host/Hostess. Similar to the companion (and many companions fulfill this ministry simultaneously), the hostesses and hosts attend to the physical and emotional comfort of the candidates. (This is sometimes referred to as "Martha Ministry," after Martha of Bethany, the sister of Mary and Lazarus, who saw to the comfort of Jesus and his disciples when they visited her home.)

These ministers are the smiling face of the local community that welcomes the newcomers. They are the parishioners who arrive early to ready the meeting space (setting up chairs, tables, candles, Scriptures; adjusting the heating/cooling; and plugging in the coffeepot). They may also be responsible for providing light refreshments, for arranging babysitting services for candidates or transportation for them, or for the myriad other details that must be attended to. This ministry, carried out well, is invaluable to the success of the entire process.

Q. Coordinating such an effort looks like a full-time job. How is any one person able to do all that?

A. The secret of success here is for coordinators *not to try to do everything themselves.* Those of us who minister in the Church need to call ourselves continually to a conversion that allows us to affirm that the Messiah has already come. Jesus has already "done it all." And the Holy Spirit is present in each baptized person; the gifts of the Spirit are also present. Our task more often than not is to call forth the gifts already present in the community and to enable those gifted sisters and brothers to make their gifts manifest. (See "Getting Started," page 100.)

3. The Process

Q. How long does the entire initiation process take?

A. That depends upon the individuals involved. Remember, the Order of Initiation is not a program into which we try to fit participants; it is a process that is shaped by the individuals involved.

We see a great variety in the types of folks who knock on our doors seeking information about and membership in the Catholic Church. This is especially true in the United States, which has no established Church and which values diversity in its citizenship. As a result, at any one time, you might find the following types of people in a single parish's inquiry group or catechumenate:

• Mary, who has never been baptized and has had no ties to a Christian Church (not baptized/no catechesis);

• John, who was baptized in the Methodist Church but has never had formal ties to, or training (catechesis) in, any Church (baptized/no catechesis);

• Michael, twenty-two, an active Catholic who was baptized as an infant, received First Communion when he was eight, was educated in Catholic schools for twelve years, but never got around to being confirmed (baptized/catechized);[3]

• Matthew, twenty-six, who was baptized as an infant in the Catholic Church but was raised in the Presbyterian Church (baptized/catechized);[4]

• Lucia, a nineteen-year-old Catholic, who was baptized as an infant but who received no religious instruction (baptized/no catechesis);[5]

• Sarah, a Jew who has attended synagogue regularly (not baptized/no catechesis in Christianity, but a "person of the Book," with faith in the one God and with knowledge of the Hebrew Scriptures);

• Timothy, a baptized, active member of the local Episcopal Church (baptized and catechized in a highly liturgical, sacramental Church);

• Jane, who was baptized as a teenager in an Assemblies of God congregation and who has attended Church and Sunday School regularly (baptized and catechized in a nonliturgical Church);

• Shaki, a member of the Yoruba people of Nigeria, who was raised in a tribe that believed in a multiplicity of gods—Olokun, the remote lord of heaven; Shango, the god of thunder; Ogu, the protector of warriors and hunters; and others (not baptized and with little knowledge of Christianity and little, if any, knowledge of the one God).

Now, this may be an improbable single group of inquirers, but it is not an impossible combination in U.S. society. Each of these individuals has very different and very special needs that must be met.

Q. But how in the world can one program hope to meet all these people where they are? How can we design a program that meets all these needs?

A. This is precisely the point. Again, the Order of Christian Initiation of Adults is not a program, so we don't have to worry about designing any one thing that will meet all the needs of everyone in this group. Let's see if we can meet each of these folks where they are. Here's how we might do that.

Let's assume that, at your parish, people inquiring into the faith are immediately invited to sit down with a member of the initiation team (this could be the pastor, director/coordinator, companion, or anyone gifted with that "easy-to-talk-to, never-met-a-stranger" ability that some folks have). This interviewer gathers the basic information (see Appendix: Sample Information and Interview Forms, page 121) and helps determine the path each inquirer will follow (always subject to revision, of course).

Ron Oakham, O.Carm., of the North American Forum on the Catechumenate, once called this the task of "sorting the fish." Referring to the gospel accounts and parables of fishing with a great net and catching all kinds of fish, Father Oakham rightly suggests that one of the first tasks of those ministering in the Order of Initiation is to "sort the fish" found in the Lord's net. In our rather diverse hypothetical group here, we find six baptized persons (John, Michael, Matthew, Lucia, Timothy and Jane) and three unbaptized (Mary, Sarah and Shaki). But a simple sorting of folks into "baptized" and "unbaptized" categories isn't really enough, because within each of these two major categories we find varying needs.

Of the baptized, for instance, we have Timothy, who, because of his active involvement in a Church very similar to the Roman Catholic Church, would most likely have fewer needs and questions than John, who, though baptized, has had no experience of, or formation in, any Church.

John's needs are much closer to the needs of Mary and Lucia, since both are uncatechized, even though Lucia is baptized while Mary is not.

Jane, Matthew and Michael, on the other hand, are all baptized and catechized, which seems to put them in a category with Timothy. But Jane's experience of Church is much different than Timothy's. Jane's background in the Assemblies of God would most likely involve a personal conversion experience, a "second baptism" in the Holy Spirit with the gift of speaking in tongues, a free-form, nonliturgical style of worship and a literal understanding of Scripture.

Michael, on the other hand, is a Catholic in all respects except for the lack of Confirmation. Matthew's experience of Church is less liturgical than Timothy's but more liturgical than Jane's.

The three unbaptized inquirers present a similar variety. Mary is, in a way, a clean slate as far as knowledge of Christianity is concerned. Her only information is probably cultural; for example, she probably has a general awareness of the Jesus stories involved with the celebration of Christmas and Easter. Sarah has the rich tradition of Judaism to draw upon, including the Hebrew Scriptures, which Christians also believe to be the inspired word of God. But Shaki, from Nigeria, has an entirely different religious background that involves, among other things, a polytheistic understanding of God.

Q. I see the vast differences, but you still haven't explained how to "handle" them. What do we do with such a variety of persons?

A. First of all, treasure them. They are invaluable gifts that God has sent to us to enrich our lives. It is not unusual for those of us involved in the Order of Initiation to have an initial reaction to a mixed bag like this as being "a problem." Not at all.

If I were the "sorter" for this imaginary group, I would probably take the following actions:

• I would guide Mary, John, Lucia, Sarah, Jane and Shaki to our parish's inquiry sessions (meetings where the most basic questions about Catholic Christianity are discussed [see "The Precatechumenate," page 22.]).

They would attend some or all of these sessions, as needed. When they have had *their* basic questions about Christianity and the Catholic Church answered, someone on the team would discern with them their readiness to enter the catechumenate for formation in the way of being a Catholic Christian (see "Discernment," page 118).

• John, Lucia, Matthew, Michael and Jane, because they have been baptized, would never become or be called *catechumens* (*unbaptized* journeyers). John, Lucia, Matthew and Jane would be *candidates* for Confirmation and Eucharist—candidates for full communion with the Catholic Church. They would attach themselves to the catechumens for support and formation. In addition, Matthew and Jane may not stay with the catechumenate as long as the others because of their histories of active Church membership. Michael would be a candidate for Confirmation.

• I would ask both Michael and Timothy to meet with a catechist on a one-on-one basis. At these sessions, Timothy and the catechist would focus their discussions on any specifically Roman Catholic questions that he might have. Michael and his catechist would discuss Confirmation as his celebration of his adult commitment to the Catholic faith.

When Timothy and the catechist have determined that Timothy is ready to be received into the Catholic Church, they would meet jointly or separately with the pastor, who, if he concurred with

16

~~their decision, would arrange for Timothy to be received at a~~
Lord's Day Eucharist. There is no reason to require Timothy to be involved in the entire formation and initiation process. He is already initiated into the Christian community through Baptism, and he has been formed in a way of Christian living nearly identical to our own. According to his conscience, Timothy may wish to make a private confession of his sins before being received into full communion (*RCIA*, 482).

• A similar discernment process would take place with Michael, his catechist and the pastor. With the permission of his bishop, Michael could be confirmed by his pastor at a Sunday Eucharist as soon as everyone involved reached consensus that he is ready to be confirmed in the faith.

As you can see, the *needs of the inquirers* determine the path they will follow toward membership in the Catholic Church. Let me repeat that: the *needs of the inquirers determine the path* they will follow toward membership. If the Order of Initiation were treated as a program, Timothy, for example, would be lumped into the group and would endure unnecessary months of meetings and waiting to come into full communion with the Roman Church.

Please be aware that frequent formal and informal interviews with the candidates are absolutely critical to competent ministering in the Order of Initiation. If the paths of the candidates are to be determined by their needs, then those pastorally responsible for the candidates must know the candidates and their needs well. This cannot be accomplished only in group settings. We must set up frequent individual interviews with each of the inquirers.

Q. Is the "quickie" procedure you're suggesting for Timothy really OK?

A. It is in strict observance of the *Ordo*, which states:

> The baptized Christian is to receive both doctrinal and spiritual preparation, adapted to individual pastoral requirements, for reception into the full communion of the Catholic Church.... In all cases, however, discernment

should be made regarding the length of catechetical formation required for each individual candidate.... (*RCIA*, 477, 478)

The national statutes on the catechumenate state:

> Those baptized persons who have lived as Christians and need only instruction in the Catholic tradition and a degree of probation within the Catholic community should not be asked to undergo a full program parallel to the catechumenate. (*National Statutes*, 31)

It is also quite in keeping with the practice of the early Church. An ancient document called the *Canons of Hippolytus*, which dates from around A.D. 500, says that "a catechumen who is worthy of the light need not be delayed by questions of time: the Church's teacher [catechist] is the person who settles this question" (*Canons of Hippolytus*, 91).

And this practice is, of course, in agreement with the Scriptures. Peter's decision to baptize Cornelius, of Caesarea, and his entire household was a "pastoral decision" that disregarded the commonly held belief in the infant Church that a pagan must first become a Jew, then receive baptism in the name of Jesus (see Acts of the Apostles 10; 11:1-18).

4. The Periods of Initiation

Q. What are the various periods of the Order of Initiation?

A. The Order of Initiation is divided into four periods:

1. Evangelization and the Precatechumenate;
2. The Catechumenate;
3. Purification and Enlightenment;
4. Mystagogy (Period of Postbaptismal Catechesis).

Q. How long do each of the periods last?

A. The period of evangelization and the precatechumenate and the catechumenate itself last as long as is necessary for each candidate.

Normally speaking, the first period (evangelization and the precatechumenate) does not have to be overly long. Inquirers leave this period and enter the catechumenate as soon as they have had their major questions answered and when the stirrings of faith and of initial conversion have begun.

The decision to enter the catechumenate should result from the mutual discernment of the unbaptized inquirer and a member, or members, of the initiation team. The *Ordo* sets forth several "markers" to help with this decision-making process: the inquirer should "feel called away from sin and drawn into the mystery of God's love" and there should be a "genuine will to follow Christ and seek baptism" (*RCIA*, 37).

(See "Discernment," page 118.)

The *Ordo* calls the catechumenate "an extended period" (*RCIA*, 75) whose length "depends on the grace of God and on various circumstances" (*RCIA*, 76). The U.S. bishops state that this period "should extend for at least one year...[o]rdinarily...from at least the Easter season of one year until the next; preferably it should begin before Lent in one year and extend until Easter of the following year" (*National Statutes*, 6).

19

However, the catechumenate itself may last several years. Again, the length of this period is *determined by the needs of the catechumen*; it is *not* determined by parish calendars, the personal convenience of the staff or team members, or for any reason other than the *needs of the catechumen*.

In normal circumstances, the period of purification and enlightenment coincides with the season of Lent, beginning with the Rite of Election on the First Sunday of Lent and ending with the celebration of the initiation sacraments at the Easter Vigil.

Mystagogy begins after the celebration of the Sacraments of Initiation and, in the United States, continues for one year.

Using the preferred time frame in National Statute 6 as a norm, an inquirer in 1994, for example, would enter the catechumenate sometime before February 16, 1994 (Ash Wednesday), and be baptized on April 15, 1995 (Holy Saturday). At that time, mystagogy (see "Mystagogy," page 38) would begin and last until about April 7, 1996. This time frame also assumes that some period of inquiry has occurred before the person was accepted into the Order of Catechumens prior to February 16, 1994.

In another example, a person in 1995 might enter the catechumenate before March 1 (Ash Wednesday), be baptized at the Great Vigil on Holy Saturday, April 6, 1996, and complete mystagogy around Easter 1997 (March 30). (See page 110 for a hypothetical calendar.)

Q. Is this length of time a realistic expectation?

A. My experience and that of the catechumens to whom I have ministered over the years tell me that yes, it seems like a very, very long time *at the beginning* of the process, but by the end of mystagogy, few would have wanted it any shorter, and some neophytes wish that the process were even longer.

As coordinators or other ministers in the Order of Initiation, we need to trust the wisdom of the Church in this matter. We need to be certain that we are meeting the needs of the inquirers (not just responding to our own needs or fears). We need to be ready to admit to them at the outset that we, too, realize that it seems like a very long time, but that we believe it's necessary and useful. Let's assure our people (inquirers, sponsors, team members and pastors) that this is a graced period, that it is time enwrapped with divine purpose.

Q. But what about special circumstances? Can exceptions be made?

A. Of course. Let me repeat once again: The Order of Christian Initiation of Adults is to be carried out to meet the *needs of those seeking initiation.* The prescriptions in the Order and the mandates of the national statutes can and should be adjusted to fit any special, individual circumstances.

The Order has not been restored for the purpose of making people jump through a series of ecclesiastical hoops. The *Ordo* contains a section (*RCIA*, 331-339) dealing with exceptional circumstances, such as sickness, old age, change of residence and long absence for travel.

However, please be aware that the Order of Initiation should not be shortened merely because it doesn't fit into someone's schedule or because someone feels that the Church shouldn't expect so much, or because of the fear that such high expectations will frighten people away. To paraphrase a popular quip, "Fear on my part does not constitute an exceptional circumstance on the part of the Church."

5. The Precatechumenate

Q. What occurs during the period of evangelization and the precatechumenate?

A. Many people would like to think of this period as two periods so that evangelization efforts would not be lost and forgotten. Generally speaking, most U.S. Catholics remain decidedly uncomfortable with evangelization. But as Thomas Morris, executive director of the North American Forum on the Catechumenate, has said, our problem is not with evangelization *per se* but with evangelism.

Rightly or wrongly, U.S. Catholics tend to equate evangelization with a style of preaching about and witnessing to the importance of Jesus Christ in one's life that is most often associated with bombastic, fundamentalistic and highly emotional Protestant preachers—be they found on street corners or on cable television channels.

This uneasiness creates a barrier to the very real demand of the gospel to proclaim the Good News of Jesus Christ to the entire world. And it remains in spite of the establishment of national and diocesan offices of evangelization and even the issuance of apostolic exhortations such as Pope Paul VI's *Evangelization in the Modern World* (*Evangelii nuntiandi*, 1975).

My experience is that many people are drawn to the Catholic Church because they have come to know one or more Catholics and they have been touched by the way those Catholics lead their lives. It is the authentic living of the gospel, day in and day out, that speaks most powerfully to people. And this is the core of evangelization as we understand it.

During the precatechumenate portion of this period, those who come to us are called inquirers. (The *Ordo* says they may be called *sympathizers* [RCIA, 39], but this term has not been used in the United States to my knowledge.) This is basically a time for information—although it should not be given over *exclusively* to the giving and getting of information. There is hospitality, continued evangelization and the beginnings of formational activities. But this period is best characterized as informational. The inquirer seeks information about the Church, and the Church, for its part, uses this period to come to know the inquirers, to listen to their stories, to tell our own stories, to answer their questions and to help them ask better questions.

This period has no fixed time limit. It may be as short or as long as necessary for the inquirer. This is often the period during which many of the "Catholic questions" are dealt with, for example: Why do Catholics pray to saints? Why do you believe that the Pope is infallible? What exactly does *infallibility* mean? Why do you worship Mary? What is the rosary? What are indulgences? What is the Mass all about?

Various communities handle this period in various ways.

Some parishes have the inquirer meet individually with the pastor, director/coordinator of the Order of Initiation or a catechist to discuss specific questions that the inquirer raises. When both the parish member and the inquirer feel that the inquirer is ready to proceed, the unbaptized inquirer would be accepted into the catechumenate; the baptized but uncatechized inquirer would be accepted as a candidate; and the baptized and catechized inquirer would be received into full communion with the Church.

Other communities set aside a particular evening each week and, in a come-one-come-all atmosphere, meet with inquirers to share stories of personal faith and of the Church and to answer the questions the inquirers pose. Inquirers continue to come week after week until they feel ready to take the next step.

Still other parishes invite inquirers to an ongoing (yes, that's right, *ongoing*, that is, meeting *each* week, year-round) series of inquiry sessions during which inquirers are given a general overview of Christianity as it is lived out in the Catholic tradition. Inquirers will join and leave these sessions at any point (joining shortly after the initial interview and moving on when their questions are answered). This is a practical approach that works well for most parishes. Such a series might look something like this:

Session/Topic

Initial Individual Interview and Orientation to the Process

1. God
2. Jesus
3. Holy Spirit
4. Church
5. Scripture
6. Sacramentality
7. Catholic Customs and Practices
8. Prayer
9. The Mass
10. Church History: Peak Moments
11. Personal Morality
12. Social Morality
13. Ministry and Mission
14. Human Destiny

Where to from here?
   Next steps in the process

Individual Interview/Discernment

Caution: If you choose to use this last approach, resist every temptation to turn these sessions into "classes" and to set up a classroom atmosphere. Do not let yourself be fooled into equating "book learning" and the discussion of theological propositions with sharing the Good News and with initial conversion.

Q. How do you avoid turning this approach into a program?

A. It has a lot to do with where you place your emphasis. While catechisms and theological propositions about God, Jesus, the Holy Spirit and the Church provide essential information, the process of initiation depends as well on an understanding of God's revelation *here* and *now* among *these* people in *this* place at *this* time.

   That kind of revelation happens when folks speak their hearts to each other and share their concerns, their doubts, their joys, their sorrows. People begin to connect their own stories with the

Big Story, that is, with God's Story, the stories found in our Scriptures. Revelation happens when we celebrate those connections in prayer and liturgy, in mission and service.

Giving people information and books is helpful and necessary. But the transmission of books and data is not the purpose of the Order of Initiation. Conversion is at the heart of what we're about.

Q. Should members of the parish who want to update themselves about the Church attend these inquiry sessions?

A. No. These people would be better served by attending adult religious education programs specifically geared to their needs and concerns.

In addition, the inquirers are better served by participating in focused sessions directed specifically to their needs and concerns.

Lumping these two groups together, while it seems to be efficient at first glance, is unfair to both groups, each of which brings an entirely different set of questions and "baggage" with them to the sessions.

6. The Catechumenate

Q. What happens during the catechumenate?

A. The period of the catechumenate is basically given over to formation through catechesis and liturgy. Where the precatechumenate was concerned with *information* and initial conversion, the catechumenate is most properly characterized by *formation* in the Christian life and the deepening of initial conversion.

Q. How is this formation carried out?

A. The "textbook" for catechesis during this period is the Lectionary, the liturgical book containing the prescribed readings from Scripture for every day of the liturgical year. Since the Order of Christian Initiation calls for catechesis that is gradual, complete, tied to the liturgical year and supported by celebrations of the word (*RCIA*, 75.1), lectionary-based catechesis (or, more precisely, catechesis based on the Liturgy of the Word) seems ideally suited to this period of the process (see "Catechetical Method," page 70).

Q. What types of ministry are involved?

A. Nearly all ministries are exercised during this period, but the primary ministries are those of catechist, sponsor, priest, liturgist and liturgical musician.

Q. What types of gifts are necessary to carry out this period effectively?

A. Catechists with an especially solid grounding in Scripture and liturgy are invaluable. The challenge of this period is to help the catechumens consistently connect their stories to God's Story as it unfolds for the Church each Lord's Day in the Scripture readings.

Catechists are also called upon during this period to preside at various rites. A solid understanding of the dynamics of liturgical action and the value of the full use of symbol and sign are required (see "Liturgical Rites," page 43).

Liturgists and liturgical musicians are also heavily involved during the catechumenal period.

Q. What rites are celebrated during this period?

A. The *Ordo* is rich with rites to be celebrated during the period of the catechumenate. The rite marking the entrance into the catechumenate is called the Rite of Acceptance into the Order of the Catechumenate. Other rites of the catechumenate may also be celebrated during this extended period (see "Liturgical Rites," page 43). These rites are optional and include:

- special celebrations of the word;
- minor exorcisms;
- blessings;
- anointings;
- the Ephphetha, the opening of the ears and mouth
- the Presentation of the Creed;
- the Presentation of the Lord's Prayer.

Q. How often should the catechumenate meet?

A. Most catechumenates meet weekly, usually while the rest of the community is celebrating the Liturgy of the Eucharist.

Following the homily, the catechumens are formally dismissed, that is, sent forth, from the assembly. With their catechist, they go to a room in the parish complex (the catechumeneon)[6] where they "break open the word" (see "Catechetical Method," page 70). Often, following the end of Mass (which, of course, has continued without them), they are joined by their sponsors and other parish team members for refreshments, fellowship and, in some parishes, additional catechesis based upon that day's Scripture readings.

Q. You mean that you don't allow the catechumens to attend the rest of Mass?

A. It's not so much a matter of *not allowing* them to be present for the rest of the Mass; it's more a matter of sending them forth with the community's blessing to further reflect on the word just proclaimed and preached within the larger assembly.

Since the catechumens are not baptized, it is not appropriate for them to remain to pray the General Intercessions (which is a responsibility of the baptized) or to attend the Liturgy of the Eucharist, at which they are not yet welcome. To allow them to stay for the Eucharist would be very much like inviting guests to your home but not letting them join you and the rest of your family at the dinner table. Actually a more accurate parallel or analogy would be to invite everyone to sit at your family table, but then not allow your guests who are not family members to eat.

Dismissing the catechumens from the Liturgy of the Eucharist is most often a problem for the members of the parish team or sponsors; it is rarely a problem for the catechumens themselves. Many catechumens hunger for the Eucharist and eagerly await the Easter Vigil when they will receive communion for the first time, but in my experience, none has ever felt as if he or she were "thrown out" of Mass. This is a fear generally felt and/or expressed by team members and sponsors (especially if the sponsor is a Catholic spouse who remains to celebrate the Eucharist).

(For further discussion of this "problem," see pages 62-65.)

Q. Doesn't the catechist also miss Mass using this approach? How does the catechist fulfill the Sunday Mass obligation?

A. In most cases, the catechist participates in another Mass at the parish on those days when she or he is facilitating the guided reflection on the Scriptures for the catechumenate.

Q. What do you do if you live in a small parish with no anticipated Mass and only one Mass on Sunday?

A. Catechists in this situation might participate in a Eucharist at a neighboring parish. If this causes an undue hardship and it is really impossible for the catechist to celebrate Eucharist, then perhaps the catechumens should not be dismissed but should meet to break open the word on a weekday evening. However, this approach should be used only as a last resort.

Q. Should candidates, that is, those who are already baptized, be part of the catechumenate?

A. Technically, unless they are uncatechized, that is, unless they have had little or no instruction in the Christian faith, they are not meant to be an official part of the catechumenate. However, most benefit from the association with the group. I often speak of the candidates "attaching themselves to" or "associating themselves with" the catechumenate. As associated members, they participate in most of the activities of the catechumens.

Nearly everyone benefits from the formation carried out and from the community established in the catechumenate. Care must be taken, however, that the candidates, the catechumens and the team members understand the difference between catechumens (who are not baptized) and candidates (who are). It is also imperative that this difference be maintained in all liturgical rites.

From a pastoral point of view, all candidates should be encouraged to attach themselves to the catechumenate—with one exception. Candidates who have been actively involved in highly liturgical, sacramental Churches—for example, Anglican/Episcopalian and most branches of the Lutheran Church—should be received into the Catholic Church just as soon as they and the parish community are ready.

The primary purpose of the catechumenate is the formation of non-Christians into the life and beliefs of Christianity as it is lived in the Catholic tradition. Except for a handful of points of doctrine and discipline, Anglicans/Episcopalians and most Lutherans are very close in belief and practice to Catholics. As the national statutes point out, individuals in these circumstances "should not

be asked to undergo a full program parallel to the catechumenate"
(*National Statutes*, 31).

Q. What is the ideal physical setting for the catechumenate meetings?

A. My concept of an "ideal setting" would be an uncrowded room within the church building (assuming that you are holding your catechumenal meeting on the Lord's Day following a dismissal rite) that has been designed for adults.

Less than ideal settings include cafeterias with long tables and metal chairs, grade school classrooms with little desk-chairs, the corner section of any gymnasium, the church's "cry room" or any room that has to be completely set up and torn down for each catechumenal session.

I've been involved in parish work long enough to realize that you would be extremely fortunate to find the ideal physical setup in your own parish. As an old song goes, "It's what you do with what you've got—and never mind how much you've got—that pays off in the end." The physical setting, of course, is always helpful, but the work of the Holy Spirit is certainly not limited by the physical surroundings.

Q. How do you convince people that a one-, two- or three-year catechumenate is necessary?

A. In my experience, the only folks who need "convincing" about a catechumenate longer than the venerable nine-month school-year model are pastors and parish team members. Never has a catechumen complained to me that the catechumenate was too long. The very people most deeply involved in the process—the catechumens themselves—realize that they may need one, two or three years to feel ready to make their commitment to Jesus Christ. If they are serious about radical conversion and embracing a new life in Jesus Christ, time is not a problem. This "problem" belongs in the same category with the "problem" of dismissal: It's essentially a problem of the parish team and not a problem of the catechumens.

If we establish year-round catechumenates, with dismissals for breaking open the word, then, under ordinary circumstances, catechumens will request Baptism at the Easter Vigil when they are ready, whether that be one, two or even ten years after they have entered the catechumenate.

Q. I just can't imagine a catechumenate lasting longer than eight or nine months. Our September-to-Easter program has always worked. Do we *really* need to change?

A. Yes. Catechumenates shorter than one year are no longer an option. Abbreviated catechumenates may be designed for individuals under exceptional circumstances. Each abbreviated catechumenate requires the approval of the bishop.

Q. What might be some reasons for seeking the bishop's permission for an abbreviated catechumenate?

A. A life-threatening illness of a catechumen or spouse would be one reason. The *Ordo* speaks of "events that prevent the candidate from completing all the steps of the catechumenate or a depth of Christian conversion and a degree of religious maturity" (*RCIA*, 331; see also 332-339; *RCIA* 370-374 discusses initiation for those in danger of death).

Q. Should Catholics who have been away from the practice of the faith and who want to return to the Church attend these sessions?

A. This is a difficult call. On the one hand, the Order seems to be "tailor-made" for this situation. On the other hand, returning Catholics, much the same as those parish members who wish to update themselves, generally have very different needs from catechumens (see page 25). Your pastoral wisdom should be called upon here.

For instance, many Catholics who have been away from the active practice of their faith are often in need of deep spiritual, emotional and psychological healing. Often their reasons for absenting themselves had to do with the infliction of deep, painful hurts. In some instances, they may feel that they were "shoved" from the Church and not listened to.

As one involved with pastoring and ministering to those in the Order of Initiation, you must determine whether the presence of such a person in the process would be good and helpful to everyone involved: the person returning, the catechumens, the sponsors, the parish in general. Occasionally, the answer is yes; more often than not, a returning Catholic's participation in the catechumenate is not the best solution for the individual or for the catechumenate.

Ideally, these folks should be guided to a specific group of Catholics who are "coming home." A national movement is afoot in the Church that is especially designed to help people return. It is called Re-Membering Church. Contact the North American Forum on the Catechumenate for more details. (See Bibliography and Resources, page 140, for the address and telephone number.)

7. The Period of Purification and Enlightenment

Q. What occurs during the period of purification and enlightenment?

A. Think of this period as a six-week retreat. In fact, the origin of the Church's observance of the season of Lent is found in the ancient initiation process.

In the early Church, an extended period of time was set aside for the catechumens to make final spiritual preparations for their initiation at Easter. Gradually, the entire community united itself with the catechumens in these preparations through prayer, fasting and almsgiving. The community members also began to use the time as a renewal experience for their own ongoing conversion.

Centuries later, when the initiation process fell into disuse, the community retained the Lenten season as its annual retreat and preparation time for the celebration of the Easter mysteries. Now, with the restoration of the catechumenate, we once again focus on the penitential and baptismal aspects of Lent as the catechumens' retreat in which the community joins.

Q. How is this immediate preparation period carried out?

A. Sometime prior to the First Sunday of Lent, an interview should be conducted with each catechumen. The purpose of this interview is to determine the readiness of the catechumen to take the next step in the process: handing in her or his name to the bishop and being chosen (elected) by the Lord through the Church community to celebrate the initiation sacraments at the upcoming Easter Vigil.

The rite marking this stage of initiation is called the Rite of Election. It is presided over by the bishop or his delegate, and it is usually celebrated in the cathedral church or, in geographically large dioceses, in the church of the local dean or vicar, or even in another church (see "Liturgical Rites," page 43). After celebrating the Rite of Election, the catechumens are no longer called *catechumens*; they are referred to as the *elect*.

In those parishes that have developed the Order of Initiation into an ongoing process, it is possible that during any one Lent the parish may be ministering to inquirers, catechumens, candidates, elect and neophytes—all at the same time. When this happens, the various designations become important in order to distinguish where each person is in the process.

In the United States, another rite has been developed for the already-baptized candidates seeking Confirmation, First Eucharist and/or full communion with the Catholic Church. This rite is called the Rite of the Call to Continuing Conversion and is combined with the Rite of Election in those instances where both catechumens and candidates are involved.

During the Lenten period, other liturgical rites are celebrated. These are called the Scrutinies (for the elect) and the Penitential Rite (for candidates).

Several optional rites may also be celebrated. One is the Rite of Sending Catechumens for Election by the Bishop; another is the Rite of Sending Candidates for Recognition by the Bishop. These two rites are combined in those communities that have both catechumens and candidates preparing for the Easter sacraments.

Because the Rites of Election and the Call to Continuing Conversion take place outside the parish, these optional rites, which are celebrated at the local parish, were developed as a way to keep the local community involved in each step of its catechumens' and candidates' journeys.

Two other optional rites may also be celebrated with the elect during this period: the Presentation of the Creed and the Presentation of the Lord's Prayer. (See "Liturgical Rites," page 43, for more about these celebrations.)

In addition to these liturgical celebrations, the elect (and candidates, where appropriate) continue to meet each Lord's Day for breaking open the word and for reflection on the meaning of the rites they are celebrating.

Many communities schedule a day of reflection or a retreat weekend during this period for the elect and their godparents, for the candidates and their sponsors and for the team members.

It is also a good idea to model the meaning of Lent for the elect and the candidates. They should be encouraged, by your example, to fast, to pray, to do penance and to give alms.

Candidates should also be encouraged to celebrate the Sacrament of Reconciliation during this time and, of course, should receive the catechesis necessary to celebrate the sacrament fruitfully.

Q. What types of ministry are involved during this period?

A. The ministry of catechist continues, of course. But during this period, liturgical ministers—priest, liturgist, liturgical musicians and so forth—are vitally important. Many rites are celebrated, and the power of the rites is best released when they are celebrated in such a way that the signs are used in their fullness.

Q. What do you mean when you say that the signs should be used in their fullness?

A. There's a tendency toward minimalism among us—a desire, for example, to use the tiniest smidgin of oil when we anoint (it's so messy, after all!), a dribble of water when we baptize (we certainly wouldn't want to get anyone all wet!), the smallest possible tracing of the sign of the cross, using the lightest touch possible when we sign a person's forehead or senses with the cross.

If the sacramental signs are to communicate and effect what they signify, then we need to employ them in the fullest way possible. Oil is meant to be felt and to be massaged into the skin. To *baptize* means to *immerse* or *to plunge into*. Let's allow the person being baptized to experience the immersion, the washing. If we are marking persons with the cross, the sign of salvation, let's really mark them, brand them as it were, with a touch that they can actually feel, using the flat of our entire hand, not merely the tip of our thumb.

Q. What other types of gifts are necessary for carrying out this period effectively?

A. Spiritual direction is important during this period. If you have parishioners who are trained and gifted in this ministry, you should encourage the elect and candidates to avail themselves of their ministry.

Godparents also come into play during this period, as do sponsors for Confirmation. (Remember, up to this time, sponsors may have been parishioners other than the godparents or Confirmation sponsors [see "Ministries," page 9].)

It is a good idea to hold inservice sessions for godparents and Confirmation sponsors several weeks prior to the beginning of Lent. During those sessions, you will want to outline the Church's expectations of their ministry roles. Be prepared to meet with apprehensive people. Many will be filled with anxiety about what is expected of them. Many fear that they will need to become instant theologians in order to fulfill their roles. Deal with that anxiety immediately.

Q. How often should the elect meet?

A. At least weekly on the Lord's Day for Liturgy of the Word, breaking open the word and liturgical rites, when appropriate.

Then there is the possibility of a day of reflection or a weekend retreat.

Other optional liturgical rites may be scheduled on weekday evenings. Minor rites, such as anointings with the Oil of Catechumens and the Ephphetha, may also occur.

Again, call upon your pastoral wisdom. The Order of Initiation is exceedingly rich with possibilities. But please remember that this Lenten preparation time is also a time for private prayer and reflection. Don't overschedule yourself, the team members or the elect and candidates. Allow time for everyone to "be still and know" that God is God.

Q. Should the elect and the catechumens continue to meet together? What about the candidates?

A. There is no reason why the elect, candidates and catechumens should not continue to meet together for Liturgy of the Word and breaking open the word each Lord's Day. The catechumens could also be specifically invited to be present for the celebrations of some of the minor rites.

It would probably not be appropriate for the catechumens to be present during a day of reflection or a weekend retreat for the elect nor would their presence be appropriate during reflection on the major rites during this period (Rite of Election, Scrutinies). Such reflections in the presence of the catechumens would tend to preempt their own, later reflections.

8. Mystagogy

Q. What is mystagogy all about? What is its purpose?

A. Mystagogy is basically a time for the neophytes, the newly baptized, to savor the meaning of the sacramental experiences that they have undergone on their journeys to initiation.

The *Ordo* sets forth these goals and purposes for mystagogy:

- to deepen the Christian experience;
- to grow spiritually;
- to enter more fully into the life and unity of the community (*RCIA*, 7.4).

And the *Ordo* says that these goals can be accomplished:

- by meditating on the gospel;
- by sharing in the Eucharist with the community;
- by performing works of charity (*RCIA*, 244).

The immediate mystagogy occurs at the so-called Neophyte Masses of the Easter season, when the neophytes and their godparents join the entire community for not only the Liturgy of the Word, but now for the Liturgy of the Eucharist, too.

After the celebration of Pentecost, the end of the Easter season, the neophytes, their godparents and companions continue to meet at least monthly with the community's mystagogue for one year.

Of all the various components of the Order of Initiation, the mystagogy is the least understood and the last to be successfully implemented.

Q. Well, that's easy to understand: We're all so tired by Easter! How can we continue with any sort of enthusiasm?

A. Don't merely continue. Expand the involvement. Find people who have not been heavily involved in other stages of the process and ask them to serve as mystagogues, musicians, liturgists, hosts/hostesses and so on for mystagogy. Remember: You don't have to do everything yourself and neither does the core team.

Q. Did you say that the neophytes continue to meet for an entire year?

A. Yes. National Statute 24 calls for a year-long mystagogy comprising at least monthly meetings.

Q. Is a year-long mystagogy realistic? We've never been able to get our neophytes to come to even a few meetings after Easter.

A. If it's never worked before, maybe it's never been approached in the right way before. If the entire process has been carried off as envisioned, a year-long mystagogy will seem too short to most neophytes. If we have failed to evangelize effectively, to catechize, build community and equip for mission, then a mystagogy that lasts for a year is impractical because no one will come.

Work at building community from the very first inquiry session. Believe in and communicate frequently the fact that conversion is a never-ending journey for everyone. Exorcize the consumerist mentality that sees the Order of Initiation as a program leading to the "purchase" of a product. The initiation sacraments are not products; they are not consumer goods; they are not "things" one "gets." Communicate from the beginning that active participation is necessary and that participation in mystagogy is among your (the Church's) expectations of neophytes. Make certain that what you are offering is substantive and perceived as needed by the neophytes. Change the pace, the setting and the team (if possible).

Q. What happens if the neophytes just don't show up?

A. Use the scheduled time for planning improvements in your process.

Q. Precisely how is mystagogy carried out? What do you do?

A. I believe that today's mystagogy should be a "savoring time," a time to sit back and think about the deeper meaning of the rites that the neophytes have celebrated during their journeys to the waters of Baptism. This should be done with a mystagogue and with the community. It is especially important for the neophytes to reflect on the rites that took place during the preceding Lent and at the Easter Vigil. (For a fuller discussion of mystagogy as a savoring time, see my book *Cenacle Sessions*, listed in Bibliography and Resources, page 140.)

You might also wish to use this mystagogic year of grace to reflect on all the sacraments, even those not specific to the initiation process (Marriage, Orders, Anointing of the Sick). You will note that during the precatechumenate period, the sample inquiry sessions did not include catechesis on any specific sacraments other than the Eucharist as it is celebrated in the Order of the Mass (see page 24).

In the early Church, the meaning of the sacraments was "unpacked" only after the sacraments were experienced. The early Church fathers understood that the sacramental experience—that grace-full encounter with the Risen Jesus—comprised more than an intellectualization of the concepts, more than a "head trip." It had to do with the heart—with emotions and with intuition. The fathers of the Church understood, therefore, that really meaningful reflection on the sacraments was impossible before a person experienced them. It is my hope that all those involved in the Order of Initiation will also come to embrace this understanding.

Take time, of course, during mystagogy to speak of mission and ministry—not specifically to "sign up" neophytes for this or that parish committee (please resist this temptation). But do spend some time unrolling for them the responsibilities they assumed at Baptism and giving them specific ideas and suggestions about just how they might carry out those responsibilities for this people at this time.

And, for heaven's sake, please take time to party, to celebrate. A verse, which some attribute to the British poet Hilaire Belloc, captures the Catholic vision of sacramentality, a vision that sees

the Creator's hand in all the things of the earth—and these things
are good:

> Wherever a Catholic sun doth shine,
> There's plenty of laughter and good red wine.
> At least I've always found it so.
> *Benedicamus Domino!*[7]

Parties, outings, cookouts, picnics and sports provide wonderful
ways to introduce the neophytes to an ever-widening circle of
sisters and brothers who are the Church.

Q. What types of ministries are involved during mystagogy?

A. The major ministry during this period is that of the mystagogue,
a catechist who specializes in postbaptismal catechesis. Other
major ministries involved in mystagogy are those of liturgist and
liturgical musician.

**Q. What types of gifts are necessary to carry out this period
effectively?**

A. Ideally, the mystagogue should be a seasoned catechist with a
basic understanding of sacramentality, which is the Catholic
vision of life that sees the Divine Presence in the extraordinarily
ordinary things of creation.

The ideal mystagogue needs to be someone especially skilled
in drawing people out. It is necessary for the mystagogue to listen
and guide the reflection rather than serve as an information-giver.

The mystagogue should also have something of the soul of an
artist and poet, someone who is able through words and through
symbolic, ritual actions to evoke vivid memories of the rites the
neophytes experienced. Because of this, the mystagogue must be
someone who was present for the rites themselves.

Q. How often should the neophytes meet?

A. The U.S. bishops, in National Statutes 22, 23 and 24, call for an
immediate mystagogy that consists of participation in the Sunday
Eucharists of the Easter season (the "Neophyte Masses") and an

extended mystagogy of "at least monthly assemblies" that lasts until the first anniversary of the neophytes' initiation.

Q. Where do the former candidates fit in? Are they required to participate in mystagogy?

A. No such requirement exists for the former candidates. Technically, they are not neophytes and should be referred to simply as "new Catholics" or the "newly received." However, if they had previously attached themselves to the catechumenate, then they certainly should be invited to participate in mystagogy. Their presence will call upon the special attentiveness of the mystagogue, who will have to be very much aware that the group will be made up of two (or even three) sets of people who have had different sacramental experiences (the three groups would be non-Christians who were baptized, non-Catholic Christians who were received and, perhaps, Catholic adults who were completing their initiation through Confirmation).

Q. What is the role of the godparents in mystagogy?

A. The godparents (and the sponsors of candidates who choose to join the mystagogy group) are welcome to accompany their godchild (or candidate). I would hope that during mystagogy the godparents and sponsors would come to see themselves as lifelong companions to those they sponsored.

9. Liturgical Rites

Q. What are the major liturgical rites celebrated in the Order of Christian Initiation of Adults?

A. The major rites are these:

- Rite of Acceptance into the Order of Catechumens;
- Rite of Election (also called the Rite of the Enrollment of Names);
- The Scrutinies (there are three, two of which must be celebrated unless dispensed by the bishop);
- Sacraments of Initiation: Baptism, Confirmation, Eucharist.

Q. What is the Rite of Acceptance and when is it celebrated?

A. The Rite of Acceptance is the liturgical celebration that marks the entrance of unbaptized inquirers into the Order of Catechumens. At this point, inquirers, as catechumens, become members of the household of Christ, although they are not full members (that is, they have not yet been admitted to the Table of the Eucharist). However, as catechumens, they have certain rights in the Church; for instance, they have a right to a Christian burial even if they die before Baptism.

This rite may be celebrated whenever the inquirer and the local community are ready. The *Ordo* calls for the establishment of an annual date (or several dates) on which to celebrate this rite. From a liturgical perspective, it is best *not* celebrated on the First Sunday of Advent, which seems to have become a favorite day for this rite in many parishes. Too much is happening liturgically on this Sunday. The addition of the Rite of Acceptance tends to overload the celebration, demanding too much of it and of the assembly. In addition, the readings for this Sunday concern the end of the world—hardly a welcoming note with which to greet new catechumens! Another Sunday seems better suited.

If you are celebrating this rite once each year, you may want to schedule it for the Third, Fourth or Fifth Sunday in Ordinary Time (in January or February). The lectionary readings for these Sundays in all three cycles speak about healing, conversion and discipleship.

Look to the rite to help you determine appropriate Sundays to choose for celebration of this rite. The *Ordo* suggests readings that may be used if the rite is celebrated on a day when the normal readings may be set aside (a weekday, for instance). The suggested readings are Genesis 12:1-4a (the response of Abram to the call of the Lord and the Lord's promise to him); Psalm 33 (praise of the Lord's power and of Divine Providence); and John 1:35-42 (the call of the first disciples).

Q. What is the Rite of Election and when is it celebrated?

A. The Rite of Election, which brings the catechumenate period to an end, celebrates the election, or choice, by God through the Church of those catechumens who will be admitted to the next celebration of the Easter sacraments. It is normally celebrated on the First Sunday of Lent, with the bishop or his delegate presiding. It is usually celebrated in the cathedral church of the diocese.

This rite is sometimes called the Rite of the Enrollment of Names because each catechumen signs his or her name in a Book of the Elect (in the early Church, it was also called the Book of Life, the Register or the *Onomatographía* [*name-writing* in Greek]). This "signing on the dotted line," so to speak, signifies the catechumen's pledge of fidelity to see the process through to full initiation. Cyril of Jerusalem, a father of the Church who lived in the fourth century, compared this action to the registration of soldiers into the army (*Procatechesis*, 1).

In the early Church, this baptismal registry was carefully guarded during times of persecution—in the wrong hands, it served as a virtual death warrant for those whose names appeared in its pages.

Q. What are the Scrutinies and when are they celebrated?

A. The three Scrutinies are solemn liturgical ceremonies of introspection and repentance. According to the *Ordo*, the Scrutinies are "meant to uncover, then heal all that is weak, defective, or sinful in the hearts of the elect; to bring out, then strengthen all that is upright, strong, and good" (*RCIA*, 141). Each Scrutiny contains an exorcism, which is celebrated "in order to deliver the elect from the power of sin and Satan, to protect them against temptation, and to give them strength in Christ" (*RCIA*, 141).

The Scrutinies are normally celebrated on the Third, Fourth and Fifth Sundays of Lent. These rites are designed to be used with the Cycle A Gospel readings for these Sundays: the Samaritan woman at the well, the cure of the man born blind and the raising of Lazarus from the dead.

According to the *Ordo*, all three Scrutinies should be celebrated, although the bishop may dispense from one of them for serious reasons. In extraordinary circumstances, the bishop may dispense from two.

Q. How can we use Cycle A readings for the Third, Fourth and Fifth Sundays of Lent during a Cycle B or Cycle C year?

A. I suspect several issues may prompt this question.

First, let's be clear that when the Scrutinies are celebrated, the *Ordo* calls for the use of the Cycle A readings for the Third, Fourth and Fifth Sundays of Lent regardless of the current lectionary cycle. There really is no option given in the *Ordo* for using the Cycle B or Cycle C readings. The reason for this is twofold:

1. The Cycle A Gospel stories for these three Sundays set the context for the Scrutinies themselves. That is, the prayers of the Scrutinies have been composed on the assumption that the Cycle A Gospels will have been proclaimed and broken open in the homily. So, to celebrate the First Scrutiny, for example, whose prayers speak of "the woman of Samaria," "thirst for living water," "worshiping in spirit and truth" and "sharing with friends and neighbors the wonder of their own meeting with Christ" without having proclaimed the Gospel account of the Samaritan woman at

the well makes little sense.

2. These particular Gospels have a venerable history of usage by the Church in conjunction with the initiation rites.

In fact, according to the general introduction to the lectionary, the Cycle A readings may be used for these Sundays of Lent even if the Scrutinies are not being celebrated. The introduction says, "Since these passages are very important in relation to Christian initiation they may also be used for years B and C, especially when candidates for Baptism are present" (Introduction to the Lectionary for Mass [*Ordo lectionum missae*], 13).

Below are some of the concerns that prompt this question and responses to those concerns.

• **Concern: the people (assembly) will be confused.**

Alert them ahead of time that something special will be taking place on the Third, Fourth and Fifth Sundays of Lent. Let them know what the readings will be if they normally prepare for liturgy by reading the prescribed Scriptures at home. If necessary, tell them that the readings are not in the missalette, or tell them where the Cycle A readings can be found in the worship aid they normally use.

• **Concern: the lectors will be confused.**

Alert them well in advance and provide them with the proper scriptural texts.

• **Concern: the homilist will have to prepare two homilies.** (This assumes that the Cycle A readings will be used only at the Mass during which the Scrutinies are celebrated and that the regular readings will be used at other Masses.)

Use the Cycle A readings at all Masses on those weekends.

• **Concern: if we use Cycle A readings for these three Sundays every year, the people will never hear the Cycle B and C readings.**

While there is much to be said for variety and for the Church's shift from an annual cycle of readings to a three-year cycle, the assembly will certainly not suffer irreparable harm from not hearing the readings of Cycles B and C on these three Sundays.

The powerful messages of the Cycle A readings, linked with a competent celebration of the Scrutinies, should more than make up for the missed readings.

In addition, there are numerous instances in the lectionary where the same, or nearly the same, Scripture passages are repeated each year because of the importance that the Church attaches to the memory of these stories. For instance, the Gospel for the Second Sunday of Easter is John 20:19-31 (the story of Doubting Thomas) in all three cycles; the Gospel for Pentecost each year is John 20:19-23, regardless of the cycle.

We need to keep in mind that, as a Church, we are returning to an understanding of Lent as the *elect's immediate preparation time* for the Easter sacraments. As a parish community, *we are joining them* in their preparation and, in doing so, we are renewing our own faith and spirituality. *The elect are not joining us for Lenten fasting, prayer, penance and almsgiving; we are joining them.* If this is so, then the "theme," or focus, of each year's Lenten observance in the parish should be the elect and their journey to death and resurrection at Easter and our own journeys with them.

Q. How do you explain the Scrutinies and prepare the elect and the parish for these celebrations?

A. The Scrutinies are best explained as liturgical rites meant to help us identify and concentrate on things in our individual lives and in our corporate life as Church that are not in harmony with the teaching found in the gospel of Jesus Christ. The words of explanation found in the *Ordo* perhaps say it best:

> The scrutinies...are rites for self-searching and repentance.... [They] are meant to uncover, then heal all that is weak, defective, or sinful in the hearts of the elect; to bring out, then strengthen all that is upright, strong and good. For the scrutinies are celebrated in order to deliver the elect from the power of sin and Satan, to protect them against temptation and to give them strength in Christ.... These rites, therefore, should complete the conversion of the elect and deepen their resolve to hold fast to Christ and to carry out their decision to love God above all. (*RCIA*, 141)

It is important to point out to the elect that, despite the name *Scrutinies*, there will be no public examination of individual consciences! It is also helpful to spend some time discussing exorcism, its meaning and its purposes in the Church. Given the spine-chilling movies of the 1970's (now being shown to a new generation on late-night television) that dealt with supposed extraordinary satanic possession in very graphic ways, the very mention of the word *exorcism* will cause raised eyebrows and elevated heart rates.

The ideal time to discuss the Scrutinies is during a day of reflection or a weekend retreat scheduled during the two weeks between the Rite of Election and the First Scrutiny. As part of that day, ask the elect to scrutinize their own lives and the life of the Church. Then ask them to list anonymously on a sheet of paper three things that they see as weak, defective or sinful in their lives and that of the Church—things that they intend to pray to be delivered from during their Lenten preparation period. Then take these listings and compose a litany of deliverance to be chanted during the Scrutinies. In this way, the entire community can unite itself to pray for the specific needs of these specific elect and of the Church. It goes without saying, of course, that the composer of the litany will couch the petitions in such a way as to preserve the anonymity of each petitioner.

Q. What are the Sacraments of Initiation and when are they celebrated?

A. The *Sacraments of Initiation—Baptism, Confirmation and Eucharist*—are normally celebrated during the Great Vigil on Holy Saturday/Easter Sunday. If you have both unbaptized and previously uncatechized but baptized persons, be certain that you observe the cautions given throughout the *Ordo* and in the National Statutes (#34) regarding the distinction that must be made and maintained between unbaptized and baptized candidates, especially those baptized individuals who have received catechesis and have been active members of other Christian communities.[8]

Q. What about the other rites?

A. Other optional rites, sometimes called the *minor rites*, consist of:

- celebrations of the word of God;
- minor exorcisms;
- blessings;
- anointings.

Q. When and how are the minor rites celebrated, what is their purpose and who presides?

A. *Celebrations of the word* may be held at any time during the entire process, but they are especially appropriate during the catechumenate proper. They may be either special celebrations for the catechumens, or they may be the actual Liturgy of the Word during Lord's Day worship with the community.

According to the *Ordo*, the purposes of word celebrations are to implant Christian teaching into the hearts of the hearers, to expose them to different ways of prayer, to situate catechesis in the context of prayer and liturgy and to allow them to participate in the seasons of the liturgical year (*RCIA*, 82).

If you hold celebrations of the word during the precatechumenate, they will help prepare the inquirers for the time when, as catechumens, they will join the assembly on the Lord's Day to listen to the word of God proclaimed.

A priest, deacon or layperson may preside at a word celebration.

Minor exorcisms may be celebrated during the catechumenate and the period of purification and enlightenment. A priest, deacon or deputed catechist (one authorized by the bishop) may preside.

Minor exorcisms are petitions to God, the Creator, who made all creatures and who loves and protects them. They are meant to draw attention to the nature of the Christian life, to the struggle we all experience between good and evil, to the importance of control of oneself and to the need for reliance on God's help in a new way of life. It is inappropriate to exorcize candidates because

49

they are already baptized.

Eleven different forms of minor exorcism are given in the *Ordo* (*RCIA*, 94), and most of them lend themselves for use in conjunction with certain scriptural passages. For example, Form D, which recalls the Beatitudes, may be used quite effectively following a reading from Matthew 5 (Sermon on the Mount) or Luke 6:17ff. (Sermon on the Plain).

If your catechumens are being sent forth following the Liturgy of the Word for continued reflection on the lectionary readings and the homily, you need to be aware of the "themes" of the exorcisms and of the blessings (see below). Linking the message of that day's Scriptures, which the catechumens are reflecting on, with the exorcism or blessing prayer is most appropriate.

During the exorcism, the catechumens are asked to kneel or bow profoundly while the presider prays over them with outstretched hands. While the *Ordo* does not call for the imposition of hands during these rites, it does call for a laying on of hands for the blessings and during the major exorcisms of the Scrutinies. So it seems an intelligent adaptation to suggest that hands be imposed on each catechumen as part of the ritual action of these minor exorcisms.

The *blessings* are signs of God's love for the catechumens and the Church's concern for them. Since the graces of the sacraments are not yet available to the catechumens, the blessings are meant to give them courage, joy and peace during their journey toward the Sacraments of Initiation.

A priest, deacon or deputed catechist may give the blessings.

To impart a blessing, the presider stretches his or her hands over the catechumens and prays one of the nine forms given in the *Ordo* (*RCIA*, 97). Again, for the most part, the forms are composed to reflect various scriptural passages. For example, Form F speaks of casting down Satan, breaking chains, the strengthening of faith and cleanliness of heart. This form would be most appropriate to use following or in conjunction with readings from Luke 4:18 or 10:18; Romans 16:20; Isaiah 42:7 or 61:1; Psalms 14:7, 85:1 or 126:1.

Caution: Some of the forms of blessing given in the *Ordo* contain specific language meant only for the unbaptized. If you are imparting a blessing to a mixed group (candidates and catechumens), you will need to choose the form carefully or adjust the language to make certain that you include the baptized candidates in the blessing.

While the *Ordo* is silent on the bodily attitude of the catechumens and candidates, it seems appropriate that the catechumens and candidates stand for the blessing.

At the end of the prayer, the presider imposes hands on each individual. If large numbers are present, then the presider should be assisted in this ritual action by a deputed catechist, or deacon and other priests, if they are present.

In the early Church, it was the custom for the catechist to impose hands on the catechumens and bless or exorcize them after each meeting (*The Apostolic Tradition of Hippolytus*, XVIII, XIX, XX.3, ca. A.D. 215; the *Canons of Hippolytus*, 99, ca. A.D. 500). This is certainly a practice that should be restored in today's Church.

Multiple *anointings* are called for during the journey to the Easter sacraments. The *Ordo* prescribes their use whenever they seem to be beneficial or desirable. In the United States, the anointings take place during the catechumenate and during the purification and enlightenment periods. It is not appropriate to anoint already-baptized candidates for two reasons: First, this is the Oil of Catechumens, and it has been especially blessed by the bishop for use with the unbaptized; also these candidates, already having been baptized, have the graces of Baptism available to them.

The purpose of the anointings is twofold: It is exorcistic and it is strengthening.

As an exorcism, it is a prayer-action that breaks whatever has bound the catechumen in the past and breaks down the opposition of the Evil One to the catechumen's embrace of a new way of life.

As a sign of strengthening, the anointing gives an added robustness to the catechumen's determination to proceed in the final steps of professing the faith and of holding fast to the faith.

The oil used for these anointings is the Oil of Catechumens blessed by the bishop at the annual Chrism Mass. Immediately before the rite and for pastoral reasons, a priest may bless oil other than that blessed by the bishop.

The presider for the anointings is a priest or deacon.

Anointing with the Oil of Catechumens usually takes place after a celebration of the word. The oil may be applied to the chest, hands, or any other appropriate part of the body. In the United States, it is customary to anoint the forehead and the palms of the hands.

After the anointing, the presider or an assistant (deacon, deputed catechist) may impart a blessing.

Q. What are the optional rites and when are they celebrated?

A. The Order of Initiation sets forth numerous optional rites that may be celebrated as pastoral wisdom dictates. They are organized here by the period in which they are normally celebrated.

Period of the Catechumenate

- Exorcism and Renunciation of False Worship
- Giving of a New Name
- Presentation of a Cross
- Rite of Welcoming the Candidates
- Rite of Sending of the Catechumens for Election
- Rite of Sending the Candidates for Recognition by the Bishop and for the Call to Continuing Conversion.

Period of Purification and Enlightenment

- Rite of Calling the Candidates to Continuing Conversion
- Penitential Rite (Scrutiny)
- Presentation of the Creed
- Presentation of the Lord's Prayer
- Recitation of the Creed
- Ephphetha
- Choosing a Baptismal Name.

Period of the Catechumenate. Three optional rites may be incorporated into the Rite of Acceptance into the Order of Catechumens. The permission of the bishop is necessary to celebrate two of them: a first *Exorcism and Renunciation of False*

Worship (*RCIA*, 70) and the *Giving of a New Name*.

This particular exorcism and renunciation of false worship is rarely seen in the United States but is appropriate in cases of the serious previous involvement of the catechumen-to-be with the occult, magic, voodoo, Santeria, witchcraft, Satanism and the like. It may also be appropriate in the case of an inquirer with a previous belief in multiple gods, in ancestor worship or in animism. The use of this exorcism and renunciation has been left to the discretion of the diocesan bishop by the National Conference of Catholic Bishops (NCCB).

The rite of *Giving of a New Name* (*RCIA*, 73) is appropriate where the inquirer is from a culture in which the giving of a new name is the custom of non-Christian religions of that culture. The new name may be a Christian name or another name that is not in conflict with Christian beliefs. In the United States, the NCCB has determined that normally a new name will not be given. However, the diocesan bishop may make exceptions to this decision when circumstances warrant.

The third optional rite that may be used with the Rite of Acceptance is the *Presentation of a Cross* (*RCIA*, 74). In the United States, the NCCB has already decided that this rite may be used at the discretion of the local community (that is, the local bishop's permission has already been given through this decision of the NCCB).

Please be aware that it is inappropriate to celebrate the first two rites with baptized candidates. The *Ordo* allows for a cross to be given to the already-baptized. However, some distinction should be made in the presentation of a cross to a baptized candidate. Some symbol or symbolic action should make the presentation to a baptized person different from the presentation to an unbaptized person.[9]

Similarly, within the celebration of the Rite of Acceptance into the Order of Catechumens and the Rite of Welcoming the Candidates (or within the combined rite), the *Presentation of a Book of the Gospels* is also optional. Some communities give the catechumens Bibles, missals or other books containing the lectionary readings. These books are especially useful if the catechumens are to be sent forth from the Sunday assembly to reflect further on the word.

Please resist all inclinations to use throwaway worship aids such as missalettes in this ceremony; better to make no presentation of the Gospels than to present catechumens with a "use-once-and-toss" booklet.

It should be noted that it is appropriate to formally present baptized Christians with a book of the Gospels only if they have received no previous instruction or formation in the Christian faith (*National Statutes*, 31). However, if you celebrate a combined rite of acceptance and rite of welcoming during which you present such a book to your catechumens and if baptized and catechized candidates decide to attach themselves to the catechumenate (see page 29), then it is most appropriate to make an informal presentation of a book of the Gospels to the candidates or to distinguish in some other way between the presentation to the baptized and to the unbaptized.

For instance, you might informally present a book of the Gospels to the baptized candidates immediately prior to the rite in whatever room or area you gather in. Then, let them come to the rites already in possession of the gospel books. During the rite, the presider could speak of their use of the books to deepen their understanding of the Good News, which they had embraced at their baptisms.

The fact that the *Rite of Welcoming the Candidates* (*RCIA*, 411) is an optional rite again brings us to the realization that the Order of Christian Initiation of Adults has been restored primarily for *unbaptized* persons wishing to enter the Christian way of life in the Catholic tradition. The Order is not meant primarily for baptized non-Catholics who wish to enter into full communion with the Catholic Church.

In the United States, many people involved in the Order of Initiation find this point difficult to understand. In this country, a majority of those we welcome are Protestant Christians seeking full communion with the Catholic Church. For most parishes in most parts of the United States, the majority of their candidates are precisely that: baptized candidates for full communion; the minority are unbaptized individuals seeking to become Catholic Christians.

However, the Order of Christian Initiation of Adults is meant primarily for the unbaptized. The inclusion of baptized non-

Catholics is, by and large, an exception, and rites have been designed to mark their particular journeys in an appropriate—but different—way than the rites that celebrate the journeys of the unbaptized.

For example, in the United States, the Order of Christian Initiation of Adults has been expanded to include a rite that would involve the local assembly, that is, the parish, in the celebration of election. This is called the *Rite of Sending of the Catechumens for Election (RCIA*, 106ff.). A similar parish-based rite was also created for sending the candidates to the bishop or his delegate. That rite is called (take a deep breath, the official title has seventeen words in it!) the *Rite of Sending the Candidates for Recognition by the Bishop and for the Call to Continuing Conversion (RCIA*, 434ff.).

Most parishes in the United States have both catechumens and candidates in the Order of Initiation process, so these rites have been combined under the title *Parish Celebration for Sending Catechumens for Election and Candidates for Recognition by the Bishop (RCIA*, 530ff.).

Since the Rite of Election and the Rite of Recognition and Call to Continuing Conversion take place outside the parish (usually in the cathedral church or in the church of the vicar of the vicariate or the dean of the deanery), this rite gives parish members the chance to voice their approval and support of the catechumens and candidates.

The rite is often celebrated in the parish on Ash Wednesday or on the morning of the First Sunday of Lent, with the diocesan rites being celebrated later that day or sometime during that first week of Lent.

Period of Purification and Enlightenment. The *Rite of Calling the Candidates to Continuing Conversion (RCIA*, 446ff.) is meant to be celebrated in a local community that has no catechumens and whose candidates, for whatever reason, are not participating in a diocesan celebration of the rite and the *Rite of Recognition by the Bishop*. The pastor of the parish presides and the rite is celebrated at the beginning of Lent, ideally on the First Sunday of Lent.

It is inappropriate to celebrate the Scrutinies with the baptized because the entire thrust of the Scrutinies has to do with final preparation for Baptism, and the language of the scrutinies uses images of Baptism. Therefore the Order of Initiation provides what it calls a *Penitential Rite (Scrutiny)* (*RCIA*, 459ff.) for celebration with candidates. This rite can be used to help prepare candidates to celebrate the Sacrament of Penance, or Reconciliation, but it should not be confused with the sacrament itself. The rite is very similar to the Scrutinies save for the fact that it contains no prayer of exorcism; however, it does direct the presider and his assistant to impose hands upon the heads of the candidates.

This rite is normally celebrated on the Second Sunday of Lent, the Sunday prior to the celebration of the First Scrutiny with the elect. It may also be celebrated on a weekday during Lent.

The *Presentation of the Creed* (*RCIA*, 147, 148, 157ff.), also called the handing over, or handing on, of the creed—the *traditio symboli* (the handing on of the symbol, or reminder, of the faith) and the *Presentation* (or handing over/on) *of the Lord's Prayer* (*RCIA*, 147, 149, 178ff., 185.2.) are often celebrated in conjunction with the Scrutinies on the Third and Fifth Sundays of Lent, respectively. However, the *Ordo* says that it is "desirable" for them to be celebrated at weekday Masses during the third and fifth weeks of Lent. The Presentation of the Lord's Prayer may also be celebrated during preparation rites on Holy Saturday.

In the Presentation of the Creed, the Church hands over its statement of belief to the elect. Having received that statement of belief, the elect ritually demonstrate that they have made it their own by giving it back to the assembled Church at a later time in a rite called the *Recitation* (the return or rendering) *of the Creed* (*RCIA*, 193ff.). It is also known as the *redditio symboli* (handing back or giving back of the symbol [reminder] of the faith, that is, the creed), and it is celebrated on Holy Saturday during the day at the preparation rites. Of course, it is only celebrated if the Presentation of the Creed was celebrated earlier.

The *Ordo* states that the "elect are to commit the Creed to memory and they will recite it publicly prior to professing their faith...on the day of their baptism" (*RCIA*, 148). This directive is not generally being followed and has led some liturgists, including Aidan Kavanagh, O.S.B., to urge that the *Ordo* be adhered to and that we return to the ancient practice of having the elect recite the creed from memory during this rite.

Please note that it is appropriate to celebrate the Presentation of the Creed or the Lord's Prayer with baptized candidates only if they have previously received no catechesis (instruction and formation) in the Christian faith (*National Statutes*, 31).

Also celebrated on Holy Saturday is the *Ephphetha* (*RCIA*, 197ff.), the rite of the opening of the ears and the mouth in order to hear the word of God and profess it boldly.

The rite, celebrated with the elect, is based on the incident in the Gospel of Mark in which Jesus cures the man who was mute and deaf by commanding that his ears be opened (*Ephphetha!*) and that his tongue be loosed. The reading of that portion of Mark's Gospel (Mark 7:31-37) is prescribed for this rite.

A priest or deacon may preside at this rite and over the other rites of preparation on Holy Saturday.

The rite of *Choosing a Baptismal Name* may also be part of the Holy Saturday preparation rites unless it was celebrated as part of the Rite of Acceptance into the Order of Catechumens earlier (see page 53).

The Ephphetha may also be celebrated during the period of purification and enlightenment.

Q. Are there times when it is best to celebrate certain rites? Are there times when the rites should not be celebrated?

A. Yes—to both questions. Here is a "schedule" that you may wish to consider. Establishing specific dates for the celebration of the various rites is one of the first things you should do as you begin to organize your approach to the Order of Initiation in your parish. Of course, choosing the dates for celebration must always be worked out jointly with the presiders and liturgists.

Rite of Acceptance into the Order of Catechumens. This rite is best celebrated on a Lord's Day in Ordinary Time—either Winter Ordinary Time or Summer Ordinary Time. There are numerous choices:

Cycle A

Sunday III	Call of the first disciples
Sunday IV	Seek the Lord; the Beatitudes
Sunday V	Don't hide your light.
Sunday IX	Do the Father's will.
Sunday XV	Receive the word.
Sunday XVII	Choose the real treasure.
Sunday XIX	"Bid me come to you, Lord."
Sunday XX	A house for all peoples
Sunday XXII	Renounce yourself; follow the Lord.

Cycle B

Sunday III	Call of the first disciples
Sunday IV	Jesus exorcizes an unclean spirit.
Sunday V	Cure of Peter's mother-in-law
Sunday XI	Kingdom grows; seeds sprout, trees are planted.
Sunday XXVIII	Sell everything and follow Jesus.
Sunday XXX	"Lord, that I might see."

Cycle C

Sunday III	The spirit of the Lord is upon me.
Sunday IV	Jesus rejected at Nazareth
Sunday V	You will catch people, not fish.

Sunday XII	"Take up your cross and follow me."
Sunday XIII	Follow the Lord now. Don't delay.
Sunday XIX	Be ready.
Sunday XXIII	Discipleship
Sunday XXVII	The power of faith
Sunday XXXI	Jesus seeks out those who are lost.

This rite is best not celebrated on solemnities of the Church year or on Sundays during the major seasons, for example, during Advent. Many parishes celebrate this rite on the First Sunday of Advent each year; this is not recommended. Advent in and of itself is rich in symbol and message; adding additional celebrations both overloads and diffuses the celebration. When the Rite of Acceptance is celebrated, it should be the main thrust and focus of the celebration.

Depending upon the size of your catechumenate, you may wish to set aside two or even three dates during the year to celebrate this rite. As you recall, the "proper time" to celebrate the Rite of Acceptance is when the candidate is ready. Scheduling multiple celebrations throughout the year allows you to do this in a planned and orderly way. It is much simpler to cancel an unneeded scheduled rite than to try to hurriedly implement an unscheduled one.

The *Rite of Election* is normally celebrated on the First Sunday of Lent. If necessary, however, it may be celebrated somewhat before this Sunday or even on a weekday during the first week of Lent. In some large dioceses (large either in numbers or in area), this rite is celebrated more than once and in more than one place. In my own archdiocese, it has been our custom to celebrate the Rite of Election of Catechumens and the Rite of the Call to Continuing Conversion of Candidates in five or six places on three or four different days. Some of these celebrations are presided over by the archbishop, some by deans in their deaneries.

The *Scrutinies* are celebrated on the Third, Fourth and Fifth Sundays of Lent. However, according to the *Ordo*, they may be celebrated on other Sundays of Lent or even on weekdays.

If the *Presentation of the Creed* and *Presentation of the Lord's Prayer* are celebrated (remember, these are optional rites), ideally they should take place during the week following the First

Scrutiny (Presentation of the Creed) and the Third Scrutiny (Presentation of the Lord's Prayer).

This sequence and timing is in keeping with the ancient practice of the Church. However, the presentations may be celebrated as part of the First and Third scrutinies; they may even be anticipated and celebrated before the Rite of Election, that is, during the period of the catechumenate proper (*RCIA*, 79, 104, 105).

The *Sacraments of Initiation—Baptism, Confirmation, Eucharist*—are celebrated at the Great Vigil of Easter. Under extreme circumstances (for example, in mission territories where those to be initiated may number in the hundreds), other arrangements may be made. However, in the United States, only exceptional pastoral circumstances (danger of death, for instance) would allow for the celebration of these sacraments at a time other than at the Easter Vigil.

Q. How do you handle persons coming to you at different times of the year? Must they wait to be "cycled" into the rites?

A. If you establish a year-round catechumenate and schedule multiple celebrations of the Rite of Acceptance, there should be no reason to put anyone on hold while you wait for the cycle to begin. The process should always be in motion. Ideally, the Order of Initiation should be something like one of those wonderful moving sidewalks at large airports—they're always on the move, doing what they do best. A person simply hops on (and off) when he or she is ready.

If we continue to run *programs* of initiation (even if we call them processes) that begin with our cultural New Year (that's sometime shortly after Labor Day or the beginning of a new academic year) and run through Easter, then new folks will have to be stored in some sort of state of suspended animation until *we're* ready to deal with them.

Under the nine-month, school-year model of the Order of Initiation, an inquirer who arrives on a parish's doorstep during Easter week will probably be asked to wait until the following September (six months!) until a new cycle begins. I find this unconscionable. How dare we tell someone whom the Lord is calling, "I'm sorry, you'll just have to wait until we're ready to deal with you."

Q. The *Ordo* and the various rites within it make a sharp distinction between the unbaptized and the baptized. Why is this so?

A. Because the Catholic Church takes Baptism most seriously. Through Baptism, a person enters into the life-death-resurrection of Jesus Christ and becomes a new person, a person who has put on the Lord Jesus, a Christian, a member of the Church. If Baptism is entered into with that intention and if water and the trinitarian formula are used, then the person baptized has in fact entered into this new life as a Christian. It makes no difference under whose auspices that Baptism took place. As Christians, we recognize the fact that a baptized person is essentially different from what he or she was prior to Baptism. And we respect the dignity of that baptized person, who is a member of the priestly people of the New Covenant.

In the Order of Initiation, the Catholic Church wishes to guard against even the appearance that it does not recognize the dignity and value of Baptism validly administered in other Churches or ecclesial communities.

Q. Doesn't the distinction between the unbaptized and the baptized result in the ritualization of a "most-favored" status to the catechumens and an ignoring of the candidates? It seems to be most evident at the Rite of Election and the Call to Continuing Conversion celebrated with the bishop.

A. It may. But if you are pastorally sensitive in planning and implementing the rites, everyone should come away from the celebrations with the sense that catechumens and candidates have different status but certainly not that one is better than the other.

The Church's insistence on maintaining the distinction between the baptized and the unbaptized is sound theologically and pastorally. It also provides catechists with a wonderful "teachable moment." There is, after all, only "one Lord, one faith, one baptism; one God and Father of all, who is over all and through all and in all" (Ephesians 4:5-6).

Q. You've mentioned dismissal of the catechumens. Our team is very uncomfortable with this.

A. As mentioned on page 28, this is usually more of a problem for the team than for the catechumens.

Q. Is dismissal really necessary?

A. No, of course not. Dismissal is not absolutely necessary. But it's a good idea. In fact, it is a wonderful idea—for several reasons:

1. It is hospitable. Since the catechumens cannot partake of the community's shared eucharistic meal, why should they remain? As mentioned previously, it seems like inviting a group of people to your home for a party and then not allowing some guests to join everyone at the table for dinner.

2. It is liturgically significant in two ways. First, the catechumens are to be formed by reading, hearing and reflecting on the word of God. In the Rite of Acceptance, the Church points out to the catechumens that "the way of the Gospel now lies open" to them and that they should set their "feet firmly on that path and...walk in the light of Christ" (*RCIA*, 52.A). In that same rite, the Church specifically invites the catechumens to "come into the church, to share with us at the table of God's word" (*RCIA*, 60).

It is most appropriate, then, that the catechumens not only be present for the celebration of the Liturgy of the Word but that they also spend time doing what the Church specifically charged them to do: reflecting on the shared word and forming (re-forming) their lives accordingly.

Second, their dismissal is, in and of itself, a most powerful sign to the assembly of the baptized. It instantly raises questions about why the baptized are permitted to stay, about the gift that the Eucharist is to them and about their appreciation of their own baptisms. This is also a teachable moment that the presider best not let slip by.

3. It makes sense catechetically. It provides a weekly gathering of the catechumens to be formed by the word proclaimed on a particular Lord's Day in a particular season or on a particular feast. It allows for logical catechesis flowing not only from the Scriptures but also from the liturgy itself. It provides a living experience of the rhythm of the Church's liturgical year—a rhythm in which the catechumens will be living the rest of their lives.

4. It establishes a year-round catechumenate, a group that new members can join whenever the local community accepts new catechumens. The catechumenate meets on every Sunday and on every major feast. These meetings become as much a normal part of the Lord's Day celebration of the community as the homily, the collection and the coffee and donuts. As surely as the local community will celebrate a 9 a.m. Mass each Sunday, the catechumenate will gather to celebrate the Liturgy of the Word with that 9 a.m. assembly. Following the homily, the presider will bless the catechumens in the name of the assembly and the larger local community and send them forth to break open the Scriptures.

Q. Who should be dismissed? Just catechumens? How about the candidates? If you don't dismiss the candidates, what happens to their formation?

A. Technically speaking, only the catechumens should be dismissed, or sent forth, for further reflection on the word. All the baptized have a right to be present at Eucharist. The Catholic discipline, however, does not welcome baptized Christians who are not in full communion with the Catholic Church to the Table of the Eucharist: They are not welcome to receive the Eucharist.

For these reasons, we encourage candidates to associate themselves with the catechumenate for continued formation. In the cases of candidates who have had no instruction or formation in the Christian faith, we insist that they attach themselves to the catechumenate.

It is assumed that candidates who do not associate themselves with the catechumenate have been part of the Eucharist in the parish for some time, have been part of parish life for a number of years or have no need of further formation. There can be instances, of course, when a particular candidate has been fully catechized and formed but needs individual catechesis in a limited area. Such a person might be asked to meet individually with a catechist at some other time.

It is important to remember that the Order of Initiation must be tailored and responsive to the individuals involved. We cannot force people into our prearranged models.

In this particular area, it is also crucial not to lose sight of the importance of, and the blessings derived from, the communal aspects of the Order of Initiation. Generally speaking, nearly everyone—baptized and unbaptized—benefits from interaction with the members of the catechumenal community. One should not let mere convenience determine the level of a catechized, baptized candidate's participation.

(See page 29 further discussion on this point.)

Q. How is the dismissal best done?

A. On a normal Lord's Day, that is, on a Sunday when no particular initiation rites are being celebrated, the presider, at the conclusion of the silent period following the homily, asks all catechumens (and candidates who have attached themselves to the catechumenate) to come forward (or to stand in their places, if they sit in a special place in the church close to the presidential chair). When the group is assembled in front of the presider at the foot of the altar (or when they are all standing), the presider may use one of two dismissal prayers (*RCIA*, 67.A or 67.B)[10] or may use his or her[11] own words.

The content and tone of this teachable moment is very nicely reflected in Form B of the dismissals provided in the Ordo:

> My dear friends, this community now sends you forth to reflect more deeply upon the word of God which you have shared with us today. Be assured of our loving support and prayers for you. We look forward to the day when you will share fully in the Lord's Table (*RCIA*, 67.B).

At this point, the group, perhaps following a catechist, leaves the assembly and reconvenes in the catechumeneon, a room apart from the main assembly area of the church, where they continue to reflect on the Scriptures guided by a catechist. (See page 30 and pages 74-88 for related discussions.)

Q. Do the rites of the Order always have to take place within the Liturgy of the Word during a Lord's Day Eucharist?

A. No. And, as a matter of fact, several are recommended to be celebrated without being connected to a Eucharist; some are meant to be celebrated on weekdays.

Of the major rites, the Rite of Acceptance, the three Scrutinies and the Sacraments of Initiation are all generally celebrated within the context of a Lord's Day Eucharist. The Rite of Election, celebrated with the bishop or his representative in the cathedral church, is essentially a celebration of the word, and it may be celebrated on a Lord's Day or on a weekday.

All of the minor rites may be celebrated outside the context of a Lord's Day Eucharist.

Many of the optional rites are celebrated as part of a major rite. For example, the Presentation of a Cross, an optional rite, is usually celebrated as part of the Rite of Acceptance into the Order of Catechumens. The Presentation of the Creed and the Presentation of the Lord's Prayer may be celebrated at a weekday Mass during the third and fifth weeks of Lent. The Presentation of the Lord's Prayer and the Recitation of the Creed may also be celebrated on Holy Saturday as part of the preparation rites.

The Order is extremely flexible regarding the when and where (and even the how, to a great extent) of celebrating the many rites. The *Ordo* recognizes the basic premise concerning initiation into the Christian faith: All are on journeys of conversion and each person is at a different place on the road. We must always *begin with the needs of the individual* and approach everything we do in the Order of Initiation from that perspective and from no other.

The Order of Initiation encourages frequent ritual celebrations. By observing these rites at times other than at the Lord's Day Eucharists, communities can extend the celebrations over a longer period of time, have more of them and focus each celebration to better meet the needs of those in the catechumenate.

(For further discussion, see the first part of this chapter.)

Q. If word celebrations may be presided over by a catechist who is not a cleric and an anointing may be performed in conjunction with a celebration of the word, then may a catechist anoint?

A. No. At the present time, the Church reserves anointing with the Oil of Catechumens to clerics. If you wish to celebrate an anointing within a word celebration, you would need to have a deacon or a priest present for the anointing. In addition, according to general liturgical law, if a deacon or priest is present for a word celebration and is prepared to preside, he should do so.

Q. Since the *Ordo* (#98) calls for a priest or deacon to be the presiding celebrant for a "first anointing," may a catechist preside at a second, and subsequent anointings?

A. No. The term *first anointing* used in paragraph 98 of the *Ordo* refers to all anointings with the Oil of Catechumens. The catechumenal oil is the first oil used in the Christian mysteries. The second oil to be used is Chrism—at the Confirmation of adults and at the Baptism of infants. The third, or "last anointing" (*extrema/extreme = last, unctio/unction = anointing*), in the sacramental life of a Christian is with the Oil of the Sick.

The Church wishes at this time in its history to reserve anointing to clerics. A passage in the Epistle of James is often cited as the reason for the restricted practice: "Is anyone among you sick? He should summon the presbyters[12] of the church and they should pray over him and anoint [him] with oil in the name of the Lord" (James 5:14).

There is evidence that in the early Church members of the laity anointed a variety of persons—catechumens, the sick and others—so the restrictions on who may anoint may very well be based on subsequent centuries of practice when most of the ministries performed by the laity were assumed by the clergy.

The reasons for the Church's position in this matter are not well stated since the Order of Initiation permits deacons as well as priests to anoint with the Oil of Catechumens. Canon law and liturgical law, however, do not permit deacons to anoint with Chrism or with the Oil of the Sick.

Q. The rubrics call for the presider to lay hands on the catechumens when imparting a blessing but not when performing a minor exorcism. This doesn't seem logical. Am I reading the rubrics correctly?

A. Yes, you are reading the rubrics correctly. However, it is surely within the scope of intelligent adaptation called for in the *Ordo* that the presider (and his or her assistants, for example, deputed catechists) at a minor exorcism impose hands on the head of each catechumen (see page 49 for more discussion of this point).

Q. Why does the Rite of Election involve the bishop? We've always celebrated this rite in the parish and we prefer it that way. Do we have to go to the rite celebrated by the bishop?

A. The Rite of Election involves the bishop because the bishop is the one officer in the local Church who symbolizes the entire Church—local and universal. Please remember that the catechumens are not just being initiated into St. Richard Parish; they are being initiated into the Christian way of life as lived out in the Catholic tradition. The bishop is the head of the local, or particular, Church (for example, the Archdiocese of Indianapolis, or the Archdiocese of Cincinnati, or the Diocese of Memphis) and, because of his membership in the college of bishops, he is the local Church's link to the Church of Rome and the Church universal.

The General Introduction to Christian Initiation points out that bishops are

> the chief stewards of the mysteries of God and leaders of the entire liturgical life in the Church committed to them. This is why they direct the conferring of baptism.... Therefore bishops should personally celebrate baptism, especially at the Easter Vigil. They should have a particular concern for the preparation and baptism of adults. (Christian Initiation, General Introduction [*Praenotanda de initiatione christiana*], Congregation for Divine Worship, January 6, 1972, 12)

According to the *Ordo* itself, the "bishop, in person or through his delegate, sets up, regulates and promotes the program of pastoral formation for catechumens and admits the candidates [catechumens who are candidates for election] to their election and to the sacraments" (*RCIA*, 12).

In addition to these reasons, it is important to note that in our tradition the bishop presides at the Rite of Election. In the first few centuries of the Christian era, the bishop presided at all celebrations of the Sacraments of Initiation. In subsequent centuries as the Church grew and as local Churches became larger and larger, the bishop delegated his role as president of the assembly to local elders—presbyters, priests—in the outlying areas of his diocese.

In our day, the Rite of Election may be—and often is—celebrated without the bishop presiding. Given the size of most of our dioceses, it is virtually impossible for the bishop to preside over a rite or even a series of rites that would include all the elect from throughout the diocese. In my archdiocese, the archbishop presides at two celebrations of the Rite of Election in the See city and one or two celebrations of the rite in different deaneries of the archdiocese each year. In deaneries where the bishop will not be present in a particular year, the parishes of those deaneries are encouraged to celebrate the rite with the dean presiding as the archbishop's official delegate.

If you have been routinely celebrating the Rite of Election in your parish, be aware that celebrating the rite with the bishop at the cathedral church will not cut your parish out of this step in your catechumens' and candidates' initiations. A special, optional, parish rite has been devised to meet the need of parish communities to be involved at this step. It is called the Rite of Sending of the Catechumens for Election (*RCIA*, 106ff.).

There are two other related rites for specific situations. If you have no catechumens but only candidates, the rite is called Rite of Sending the Candidates for Recognition by the Bishop and for the Call to Continuing Conversion (*RCIA*, 434ff.).

If you have both catechumens and candidates, the rite is an optional, combined rite called the Parish Celebration for Sending Catechumens for Election and Candidates for Recognition by the Bishop (*RCIA*, 530ff.).

(See information on optional rites, page 55.)

Q. The *Ordo* calls for catechists to "have an active part" in the rites. How is this to be done?

A. Catechists are permitted by the *Ordo* to perform minor exorcisms and blessings if they are so deputed by the bishop. Additionally, they may preside at celebrations of the word.

Liturgists at the parish level should study the rites carefully and make intelligent adaptations. For example, catechists could assist the priest or deacon in the laying on of hands during the Scrutinies and the Penitential Rite (Scrutiny).

The *Ordo* itself calls for the involvement of catechists as well as sponsors in the signing of the senses and of the hands and the feet during the Rite of Acceptance into the Order of Catechumens and the Rite of Welcoming Candidates.

10. Catechetical Method

Q. What are the major adult learning principles that I need to know if I'm to minister effectively in the Order of Christian Initiation of Adults?

A. Adults learn differently than do children, and catechists ministering to adults must make the shift.[13]

First of all, it's most important that catechists adopt a certain overall stance, a certain mind-set, as it were, when approaching their ministry among adults, who are their peers. Primarily, catechists should *recognize the learning situation as a we-situation*. It is collaborative and wholistic—that is, all of us (catechist, team, inquirers, catechumens, companions and others) are involved and our entire selves (not just our minds, but our bodies, emotions, spirits and histories as well) are involved. An us-and-them attitude has no place in adult learning; it certainly has no place in the Order of Christian Initiation of Adults.

Once this basic "we" mind-set is in the very marrow of a catechist's bones, then other obvious principles about adults and adult learning unfold logically.

Adults are independent, not dependent, learners. Adults are capable of learning on their own. They need to be part of the process itself. What they need most from a catechist is guidance, exposure to the most appropriate and most helpful resources, tips on getting to the heart of the matter. A competent catechist will respect an adult as a mature, experienced, responsible peer who brings unique gifts to the journey that we are all traveling together.

Adults are self-directed rather than other-directed. Adults will pursue a subject they want to learn about as the knowledge leads them on. They do not need, nor do they appreciate, over-direction. Learning is *shared among* adults rather than transmitted from a teacher to a student.

Adults tend to be interested in solving problems. Adults are practical in their approach to learning. They want to apply what they learn: How is this knowledge going to help me? What relevance does this information have for my life? For the life of the community I belong to?

Adults tend to know what their needs are. Adults don't go into learning situations with "blank slates." They are experienced; they can be sources of learning for each other; they can even be sources of learning for the catechist. (Imagine that!)

Adults participate in learning situations for many, many reasons. In years of working with adults in the Order of Initiation, I've marveled at the many motives that bring adults to, and sustain them during, the initiation process. When I was new in this ministry, I would often fret a bit about what I, in my wisdom, considered less-than-pure motives for some inquirers' involvement in the process. Age and experience have certainly tempered my attitude.

I no longer fret about anyone's motivation. I tend to recognize each individual's initial reason for being present as a graced leading by the Lord. In fact, I now observe this phenomenon closely because I have found that it clarifies and demonstrates for me the work of the Holy Spirit in drawing people to God through Jesus and through the ordinary situations of life.

So, from an adult-learning point of view, the competent catechist working with adults will strive to meet learners where they are and capitalize on the various reasons why adults present themselves at inquiry and catechumenate sessions. Cherish the multiplicity of motives that draw them into the Lord's love.

Most adults will not attend every session you schedule. Don't expect them to. Everyone's life is busy; certain topics may not appeal to everyone every time; sometimes folks just need to take a break. While regular attendance is an important indicator of interest and commitment on the part of the adult learner, please don't make perfect attendance an expectation; if you do, you'll be disappointed.

Even for the things we hold very important in our lives, it will not always be possible to be present each time. Keep in mind that, in the Order of Initiation, we are most interested in formation and conversion; the acquisition of, or exposure to, information, while part of the entire process, is not the major focus or the primary purpose of the process.

Adults expect physical comfort. This can be something of a problem in most U.S. parishes, whose physical facilities tend to be designed with only schoolchildren in mind—classrooms, little desks, long narrow cafeteria tables, hard metal chairs.

In an ideal world, our parishes will begin constructing adult learning spaces—quiet, carpeted, private rooms, flexible in setup, with comfortable, adult-sized furnishings, audiovisual equipment and refreshments areas. Until that time arrives, we must do the best we can. Your creativity will be challenged in your efforts to create adult space in most parishes.

(For more information regarding adult learning techniques and principles, see Bibliography and Resources, page 140.)

Q. How do adult learning principles apply to the precatechumenate period?

A. The precatechumenate should emphasize:

- Evangelization
- Hospitality
- Basic information

Evangelization. This is a time to tell our stories and speak our hearts, unashamedly proclaiming the Lordship of Jesus in our individual lives and in the life of our community. Who is this Jesus? And what difference does Jesus make in my life, in your life and in the life of this family we call the Church?

Hospitality. Obviously, this is a time for the inquirers to come to know us, the Church. This is also a time for us to get to know the inquirers, to listen to their stories, to let them tell us about their joys and sorrows, their hurts, fears, hopes and expectations.

Our approach should be genuine and should tell inquirers: "You are welcome here at St. Richard's. We follow Jesus, who welcomed everyone into his life. We'd like to think we do the same...at least we try."

Inquirers need to know that there is only one stupid question—the one they never ask. We need to let inquirers know from our very first encounter with them that they are free to ask us any question, that no question is "off limits."

From our side, we need to be able to listen and respond to challenges such as "Prove to me that God exists" or "If God is so good, why is there so much evil in the world?"

We also need to be able to accept off-putting questions such as "Why do you worship Mary?" "Why do some preachers call the Catholic Church the Whore of Babylon?" "Why do you Catholics believe that you can buy or earn your way into heaven?" or "Why does the Catholic Church hate women and homosexuals?"

Basic information. Some leaders in the Order of Initiation have taken so heartily to the concept of so-called lectionary-based catechesis (see page 74) that they begin using the readings of the lectionary as a basis for catechesis even at this initial stage.

My experience has convinced me that the precatechumenate is not the time for catechesis based primarily on the lectionary. Such an approach seems premature here. This is the time, however, to be evangelizing the inquirers by recounting the "Big Stories" of our Scriptures. It is a time to answer inquirers' *basic* questions about being Christian, about the Catholic way of being Christian, about what difference that makes in our lives and about what difference that could make in their lives.

(See "The Precatechumenate," page 22, for more discussion.)

Q. How do adult learning principles apply to the catechumenate period?

A. All the principles should continue to be applied. In the catechumenate period, we use the scriptural readings from the lectionary (see lectionary-based catechesis below) to open up discussion of our stories—the ways God works with all of us to bring us to salvation.

The important point here is that the catechist has established an atmosphere of openness to, respect for and solidarity with the catechumens and candidates; it should be an atmosphere in which each person is a sharer and a listener. The catechist and team members, especially in the beginning, should assume a primary role of listener and only a secondary role of sharer.

The catechist facilitates discussion by asking and eliciting questions and serves as a resource for further learning.

Q. How do adult learning principles apply to mystagogy?

A. Again, the principles continue to be applied with only slight adjustment in emphasis. Although the mystagogy period chiefly stresses reflection on the sacramental events of the Order of Initiation, especially those of the initiation sacraments themselves, it is also a time for integration into the local community through mission.

Take time during mystagogy to help the neophytes reflect on the entire initiation process itself. It is a time to look back not only on what they have learned but on how they have learned—sharing, listening, journeying together. This will allow the neophytes to continue to learn and grow as Catholic Christians throughout the rest of their lives.

Q. What is lectionary-based catechesis?

A. First of all, it's something of a misnomer. What has popularly become known as lectionary-based catechesis should, according to James B. Dunning, president of the North American Forum on the Catechumenate, more accurately be called liturgical catechesis or catechesis on the Liturgy of the Word. This type of catechesis consists of formation and instruction that flows from the weekly scriptural readings proclaimed at the Lord's Day Liturgy of the Word, from the homilies on those Scripture passages, from the liturgy itself, from the rites of the Order of Initiation and from the liturgical year.

It is perhaps most simply understood if you envision a catechist using the lectionary rather than the catechism as the basic textbook for catechesis. But that is only the beginning point. It is more than that.

Caution: Catechesis on the Liturgy of the Word does not mean forcing dogmas from the scriptural selections. For example, it is most difficult for a catechist, bent on explicating the Church's teaching about papal infallibility, to connect this teaching directly with a scriptural reading. This is a misuse of the lectionary and it tends to be a fundamentalistic approach to Scripture. In its best tradition, the Catholic Church has not been one to search for "proof texts" in Scripture to defend or bolster a particular doctrinal point.

Q. But why liturgical catechesis? What's so important about this approach?

A. Among the purposes of using the Liturgy of the Word as the basis for catechesis is our recognition that the Scriptures are an "unfailing source of the spiritual life, the basis of all Christian instruction and the very kernel of theological study" (Paul VI, *Apostolic Constitution on the Roman Missal [Missale Romanum]*, April 3, 1969).

In addition, catechesis that flows from the celebration of the liturgical year "unfolds the whole mystery of Christ from the incarnation and nativity to the ascension, to Pentecost and the expectation of the blessed hope of the coming of the Lord" (*Constitution on the Sacred Liturgy [Sacrosanctum concilium]*, 102).

Liturgical catechesis, that is, catechesis based upon the Liturgy of the Word, provides catechumens with the core of Christian belief and practice; it continues the link between God's covenant with Israel and God's covenant with the new Israel, the Christian Church; it immerses the catechumens in the liturgical life of the Church.

It is vitally important that catechumens be formed in a liturgical spirituality through living the rhythm of the liturgical year. According to the Second Vatican Council, the liturgical year recalls

> the mysteries of the redemption, opens up to the faithful
> the riches of [the] Lord's powers and merits, so that these
> are in some way made present for all time; the faithful lay
> hold of them and are filled with saving grace.... In the
> various seasons of the year and in keeping

with...traditional discipline, the Church completes the
formation of the faithful by means of pious practices for
soul and body, by instruction, prayer, and works of
penance and mercy. (*Constitution on the Sacred Liturgy,*
102, 105)

Q. How is liturgical catechesis carried out? What exactly do you do?

A. There are many methods for carrying out liturgical catechesis.
It can take place on a weekday evening, but it is perhaps best done
as part of the catechumenal gathering following the catechumens'
being sent forth from each Lord's Day assembly. A typical session
might look something like this:

After the dismissal, the catechumens, accompanied by a
catechist, leave the assembly and reassemble in a space apart from
the congregation. Here, the day's Scriptures are proclaimed again.
This should be done slowly and reflectively. It is best done with
the sense that these sessions *continue* the Liturgy of the Word.

The sessions should take place in the context of continued
liturgical prayer. So, it is helpful if the lectionary is enthroned,
surrounded by candles and flowers and, perhaps, reverenced with
incense. Ritual actions should be part and parcel of these
gatherings. Catechists should certainly employ the minor rites of
the Order of Initiation—blessings, minor exorcisms, anointings, as
appropriate (see the discussion of the minor rites, page 49 ff.).

During these sessions, some communities proclaim the
Scriptures as many as three times—with periods of silence
between each reading—before the oral reflection of the group
begins. Since the catechumens have already heard the Scriptures
proclaimed once within the assembly, one proclamation here
should be sufficient. (If you choose to hold these sessions on a
weekday evening, then perhaps two, or even three, proclamations
might be necessary before engaging the group in shared
reflection.)

Some catechumenates concentrate on the Gospel for the day;
others use both the first reading (usually from the Hebrew
Scriptures) and the Gospel; others use all three readings: the first
reading, the lesson from the Christian Scriptures (usually from the

epistles) and the Gospel; still others proclaim and reflect upon all three readings and the psalm. The number of readings you choose to work with depends to a great extent upon the amount of time within which you have to work. However, if at all possible, the first reading and the Gospel should *always* be used.

The liturgists who organized our lectionary carefully chose the Gospels and the first readings not merely to reinforce each other or to provide a "theme" for each Mass but to retell the story of God's passionate love affair with the people of God. The lectionary readings are meant to reveal God's love and mercy being poured out upon us as individuals and as a people.

The Scripture passages (pericopes), found in the lectionary unfold for us God's saving relationship with a people throughout the ages. The God of Abraham, Isaac, Jacob and Moses is also the God of Jesus, Peter, Paul, Mary, Mary Magdalene, James...and us!

As Christians, we believe that God's saving interaction with the Hebrew people met its climax in Jesus of Nazareth and continues to this very day through the presence and activity of the Holy Spirit in each believer, in the Church as a group of believers and in the world.

So, it is most important to maintain the continuity of God's story through the ages. Let's not break up the unity of God's word by focusing only on the Gospel reading. If we do this, we are neglecting half the story.[14]

After proclamation of and silent reflection on the Scriptures, the catechist engages the group in "breaking open the word." One catechist I know first asks if anyone has any clarifying questions about any of the readings—what certain words mean, what the context of the reading is, what the historical circumstances might be, and so forth. When these points are cleared up, then sharing begins.

A competent catechist who works with adults should be a person who is especially gifted in drawing individuals into meaningful dialogue. This is most easily done by posing specific questions to the group that will elicit responses and further fuel the discussion. The goal here is to help each member of the group connect the scriptural stories with his or her personal story and, importantly, with the story of the Church.

And the Church I'm speaking of here is not "out there" or in

Rome. The Church I'm speaking of is that group of people at this particular time in this particular parish in this particular diocese, which is in communion with the other parishes and dioceses throughout the world and especially with the Church of Rome.

It is most important that members of the group be led beyond relating the Scriptures only to themselves. The question "What does this scriptural passage mean to me?" is an important question. But it is only part of the larger question: "What does this Scripture passage mean to the Church, to me and to each one of us and to all of us as Church?" Sometimes this approach is spoken of in terms of connecting the Big Story (found in the Scriptures) with my story (found in an individual's life experiences) and with our story (found in our community life as Church).

Caution: These sessions should be conducted in such a way that the participants are free to choose the depth at which they wish to share. A seasoned catechist will pose questions for the entire group and will rarely direct a specific question to a specific individual. In addition, the temptation to ask a question and then do a "whip-around" (proceeding around the table or circle so that each person is expected to respond) should be avoided.

Ideally, because this breaking-open-the-word session should be a continuation of the Liturgy of the Word, the catechist should work with a pastoral musician. Song should be an integral part of each session.

Other activities involved in the session are limited only by the catechist's imagination, the time available and the gifts and variety of the ministers involved. For instance, some catechists reserve ten or fifteen minutes of each session for discussion of Catholic belief and practices; others may have a "Saint of the Week" time, when they tell the group about a saint whose memorial will be celebrated during the upcoming week.

It is important to understand that liturgical catechesis or catechesis on the Liturgy of the Word is not meant to limit catechesis to the specific scriptural readings for that week. The Scriptures form the core, or heart, of the catechesis for most sessions, but not necessarily for *every* session.

Q. What is the key to connecting an individual's story to the Big Story and to our story?

A. One key is the understanding that the catechist has of her or his ministry. Catechists, especially those who minister to adults, must come to understand themselves primarily as storytellers rather than as information-givers. The Scriptures, by and large, are wonderful stories of God's relationship with God's people. Good storytellers are considered "good" simply because they really believe in their stories and the power of their stories. They thus engage the imaginations of their listeners. In doing so, they pull them into the story itself.

A storyteller-catechist will enable those in the catechumenate to enter into the story and to begin to see the bigger picture: that God's love affair with humanity in 1000 B.C. is the same love affair that is going on between God, each individual and the community of God's people in A.D. 1993.

Q. How is this done?

A. Various techniques can be used. In general, a storyteller-catechist helps the catechumens approach the Scriptures not necessarily seeking information, but asking questions. Such a method might look like this:

St. Richard Parish
Meeting of the Catechumenate
Fifth Sunday of Ordinary Time, Cycle C

Hebrew Scripture: Isaiah 6:1-2; 3-8 (Call of Isaiah)

In the year King Uzziah died, I saw the Lord seated on a high and lofty throne, with the train of his garment filling the temple. Seraphim were stationed above.
   "Holy, holy, holy is the Lord of hosts!" they cried one to the other. "All the earth is filled with his glory!" At the sound of that cry, the frame of the door shook and the house was filled with smoke.
   Then I said, "Woe is me, I am doomed! for I am a man of unclean lips, living among a people of unclean lips; yet my eyes have seen the King, the Lord of hosts!" Then one of the seraphim flew to me, holding an ember which he

had taken with tongs from the altar.

He touched my mouth with it. "See," he said, "now that this has touched your lips, your wickedness is removed, your sin purged."

Then I heard the voice of the Lord saying, "Whom shall I send? Who will go for us?" "Here I am," I said, "send me!"

Gospel: Luke 5:1-11 (Call of the First Disciples)

As the crowd pressed in on Jesus to hear the word of God, he saw two boats moored by the side of the lake; the fishermen had disembarked and were washing their nets. He got into one of the boats, the one belonging to Simon, and asked him to pull out a short distance from the shore; then, remaining seated, he continued to teach the crowds from the boat. When he had finished speaking he said to Simon, "Put out into deep water and lower your nets for a catch." Simon answered, "Master, we have been hard at it all night long and have caught nothing; but if you say so, I will lower the nets." Upon doing this they caught such a great number of fish that their nets were at the breaking point. They signaled to their mates in the other boat to come and help them. These came, and together they filled the two boats until they nearly sank.

At the sight of this, Simon Peter fell at the knees of Jesus saying, "Leave me, Lord, I am a sinful man." For indeed, amazement at the catch they had made seized him and all his shipmates, as well as James and John, Zebedee's sons, who were partners with Simon. Jesus said to Simon, "Do not be afraid. From now on you will be catching men." With that they brought their boats to land, left everything, and became his followers.

The catechist would begin this session by reading the story of the call of Isaiah to the Lord's service as prophet to Israel. (In order to catch the technique of how to read Scripture as story effectively, visit a kindergarten or primary grade school classroom during story time and observe how the teacher "reads" the story to the children.) Then the catechist should put the lectionary down and allow a few minutes of silence.

After an appropriate amount of time, the catechist returns to the lectionary and reads the Gospel for the day, allowing some silent time following the reading. Then, in a meditative way, the catechist begins to retell the story from the point of view of one of the characters in the passage.

(Note: In this example, the catechist has decided beforehand to concentrate on the Gospel reading. At another time, the catechist might wish to focus on the reading from the Hebrew Scriptures. In that case, read the passage from the Hebrew Scriptures, then read the Gospel. Then return to the first reading and retell that story. Allow appropriate periods of silence between readings.)

Returning to our example, let's suppose that, in the meditative retelling, the catechist speaks as one of the people in the crowd who had been listening to the strange rabbi named Jesus, the carpenter's son from Nazareth.

The catechist makes the scene come alive, pausing to fill in imaginative details—the way the wind blew in from the lake, warm and smelling of fresh water and fish; how he was jostled by the crowd as they pressed forward to get nearer to Jesus to hear what he was saying; what the man Jesus himself looked like; how surprised the big fisherman named Simon looked when the rabbi got into his boat and started giving him instructions on how to fish. Was Simon as surprised at this as Isaiah was at the unexpected vision he experienced some eight hundred years before?

The catechist continues in this manner until the story of the Gospel passage is finished, making links, where appropriate, to the account of Isaiah's call and response. As the story is being retold "from inside" as it were, the catechist poses questions as they occur to him or her:

• Now what would a rabbi know of fishing?

• Why would Simon agree to put out and cast his nets at Jesus' suggestion?

• What kind of a relationship did they have with each other?

• Did Simon know Jesus?

• Was this their first meeting?

• How did Simon and his partners James and John, the Bar-Zebedee brothers, feel when they made the great catch of fish—so many that "they filled the two boats until they nearly sank"?

- And what, in heaven's name, did Jesus mean when he said that Simon, James and John would begin catching people rather than fish?

- How could they just abandon their boats and begin following Jesus?

- Did Simon, James and John wonder if this was how Isaiah felt, when he stepped forward and said, "Here I am, Lord, send me"?

- What did Zebedee think of this?

- What had gotten into his two sons?

- How would these men live without any visible means of support?

At this point, the catechist would allow a longer period of silence—time for everyone to ponder some of the questions raised. Then, the catechist might pose general questions to the group—questions that will allow those present to begin to connect the Big Story with their stories and with our story:

- Has anyone here ever made abrupt major decisions about life or school or career?

- Isaiah reluctantly stepped forward to answer the call of the Lord to service. But he did so in the midst of a mystical vision at liturgy in the Temple. Was that easier for him to do than the first disciples' response to Jesus in the midst of a fishing expedition on the Lake of Gennesaret?

- Simon, John and James "left everything" to follow Jesus. Do you think Jesus is asking the same thing of each of us? Or does Jesus just ask that of priests and sisters?

- Jesus is calling each one of us to follow him. What does that mean to you? Tell us how you feel yourself called to follow the Lord?

- Do you ever think of yourself as having been caught in Jesus' net? How did that happen?

- The Church has been "casting its nets" about for two thousand years. Today we call this *evangelizing*. What do you think is the best way to evangelize?

Ideally, the catechist should only have to ask one or two questions, here and there, to generate and then guide the discussion.

The catechist would be prepared to guide a specific discussion about how discipleship is realized in the Church today...about missionary activities...about vocations to full-time service to the Church as a priest, vowed religious, or layperson...about service opportunities in the parish...about the post-Vatican II renewed emphasis on the ministry of all the People of God...about....

The point here is that the discussion will go where the Holy Spirit leads it. That doesn't mean that the catechist arrives unprepared, but it does call for a high degree of comfort with unstructured formats.

Catechesis on the Liturgy of the Word is not, at least in my understanding, a reading of the Scriptures followed by a prepared lecture by the catechist that develops the "theme" of the readings to focus on a particular doctrine. That sort of approach is much too limiting for what we should be about in the catechumenate.

Q. How long should each session last?

A. There is no "right" answer to this question. In some communities, the session lasts about thirty minutes—only as long as Mass lasts. When the Liturgy of the Eucharist ends, the sponsors, companions, spouses and children of the catechumens come to the catechumeneon, the room where the session is taking place, and meet their catechumen for coffee and donuts and for the trip home.

Other communities that dismiss their catechumens at the end of the Liturgy of the Word serve refreshments and socialize for the thirty minutes that it takes for the rest of the parish community to celebrate the Liturgy of the Eucharist. After Mass has ended, sponsors and companions join the catechumens for breaking open the word.

Still other communities spend the first thirty minutes or so in group prayer or silent meditation with the catechumens, beginning the catechetical part of the session only after Mass has ended and the sponsors and companions have joined the group.

Maureen Kelly, in an introductory essay found in *Breaking Open the Word of God*, Cycle C (see Bibliography and Resources, page 140), suggests a typical Sunday agenda that looks like this:

9:30	Gather and celebrate the Liturgy of the Word with the assembly, with dismissal after the homily
10:00	Coffee and rolls
10:10	Prayer, meditation, discussion
10:30	Sponsors and companions join the catechumens when Liturgy of the Eucharist ends
Noon	Closing prayer and dismissal[15]

This seems quite long to my mind. It expects quite a lot from catechumens, sponsors and companions to be present for two and a half hours each Sunday, year-round. The other possible problem with this schedule is the interruption for refreshments between the Liturgy of the Word and prayer, meditation and discussion, which again is interrupted when the sponsors and companions join the group at 10:30. I would prefer a schedule that looks something like this:

9:30	Gather and celebrate the Liturgy of the Word with the assembly, with dismissal after the homily
10:00	Procession to the catechumeneon; continue the Liturgy of the Word through prayer, song, discussion
10:30	When Liturgy of the Eucharist ends, sponsors and companions join the catechumens for the closing prayer and blessing, followed by coffee, rolls and socializing.

To some, this schedule may seem time-starved. However, if we're totally honest, we already know that there will never be enough time to do what we really want to do. And, let's also remember that most of the folks will be meeting each Lord's Day for more than a year, so the total meeting time over some sixty weeks is probably more than the total meeting time of a group that meets for ninety minutes each week under the nine-month academic-year approach.

Each community, however, needs to decide on the details of its own process *based upon the needs of the participants*. Only on the local level can decisions be made about what will and won't work for this group in this place at this time.

Q. Isn't lectionary-based catechesis soft on doctrine?

A. I don't believe so, but this is certainly a concern of many people.

First, let's keep in mind that we are meeting with the catechumenal group over a period of at least one year, one or more times each week. During this time, the catechumens and candidates are also participating in the Liturgy of the Word, continuing that liturgy following the dismissal from the assembly, living the liturgical year and participating in the many and varied rites of the Order of Initiation. All of these things contribute to catechesis about what we believe.

In addition, as Jim Dunning has pointed out, "We should be clear that catechesis during the Catechumenate is sacramental formation for initiation and not exposure to the entire Christian/Catholic heritage. The former happens at the beginning of the journey. The latter is the ongoing conversion journey of a lifetime" ("Dunning's Corner," *Forum*, Volume 8, Issue 4, Fall 1991, p. 2).

Pope Celestine I, in the early fifth century, said that the rule of prayer determines the rule of faith (*Legem credendi statuit lex orandi*). In other words, "If you want to know what we believe, just take a look at how we worship." In that worship, our beliefs are ritually lived out; they are enfleshed, so to speak. So, the Order's emphasis on the liturgy and the pastoral practice of liturgical catechesis, if adopted and implemented, will ensure that doctrine is both taught and "caught."

In addition, if catechesis on the Liturgy of the Word is carried out effectively, it cannot help but deal with doctrine. In the example above, the discussion of the Hebrew Scriptures and the Gospel passage for the Fifth Sunday of Ordinary Time (C) guided by a seasoned catechist, could quite naturally flow into catechesis on one or more of these "doctrinal" and "Catholic" topics:

discipleship, vocations, priestly celibacy, vowed religious life, abandonment to the will of God, mysticism, the call to reliance on Divine Providence, the role of Holy Providence, the divinity of Jesus, evangelization, the need to listen to God, discernment of God's will in one's life and other topics.

I appreciate the concern that people have about liturgical catechesis; in fact, I was several years coming to my own acceptance of this approach. However, my experience is that, done correctly, this ancient catechetical method is most powerfully effective in appropriately forming and informing all those involved.

One key to ensuring that liturgical catechesis is not "soft on doctrine" is to make certain that catechists and catechumenal groups move beyond a "me-and-the-word" approach. Catechesis flowing from the Liturgy of the Word must be more than discovering what a particular scriptural passage means to me. We must move from connecting the Big Story to my story to connecting the Big Story to *our* story. We must come to see the liturgy itself and the rites themselves as catechetical. And we must immerse ourselves in the liturgical year in order to develop a sound liturgical spirituality. When all these aspects come together, sound formation in the basic tenets of our faith will occur.

Q. The example you give is all right as far as it goes, but people also want to know about Mary, the pope, papal infallibility, the rosary, fasting and so on. How are you going to cover these important "Catholic" things by using only the lectionary?

A. First, let's remember that no one has said that all catechesis must come only from the lectionary. The lectionary is the basic textbook, but it is not the only one. Other appropriate resources can and should be used (see Bibliography and Resources, page 140). The Catholic questions will come up and, when they do, they should be dealt with.

But this is quite a different approach than our deciding for the catechumens and candidates in advance what they want or need to know about the "Catholic things" and then proceeding to design a program that will give them this information in (to our minds) an organized, logical and scheduled way. It seems to me that this approach primarily meets our need for them to know certain things that *we* believe are important.

Each of the topics mentioned in the question above could, should and would be dealt with during a year-long catechumenate that uses a liturgical approach to catechesis. Appropriate opportunities abound in our liturgically rich Church. Just look:

The role of Mary in our salvation and the rosary as a prayer form could very naturally and effectively be discussed on any of these great solemnities: Mary, Mother of God; the Annunciation; the Assumption; the Immaculate Conception; during Advent, especially on the Fourth Sunday; the Solemnity of the Epiphany. In the United States, December 12 is observed as the memorial of Our Lady of Guadalupe, an especially important feast in the Hispanic community. Introducing catechumens to the rosary would also be appropriate in May or October. (During October, the Church liturgically celebrates the memorial of Our Lady of the Rosary.)

The role of the pope and papal infallibility might be taken up around the solemnity of Peter and Paul (June 29) or the feast of the Chair of Peter (February 22), or when the Gospel readings feature Peter (Matthew 16:13-20, for example). The Roman calendar contains eleven memorials of popes: Fabian (January 20), Pius V (April 30), Sixtus II (August 7), Pontian (August 13), Gregory the Great (September 3), Cornelius and Cyprian (September 16), Callistus I (October 14), Leo the Great (November 10), Clement I (November 23), Damasus I (December 11) and Sylvester I (December 31). All would provide occasions to catechize the group on the Petrine ministry, the ministry of the pope in the Church.

Another opportunity for this catechesis would be on the Feast of the Dedication of the Church of St. John Lateran (November 9), the cathedral of the Diocese of Rome and the "mother church" of the entire Latin Rite.

Catechesis on fasting, of course, could take place just prior to Lent and could be revisited on Ash Wednesday or the First Sunday of Lent.

Liturgical catechesis is not soft on doctrine. In fact, because it tends to deal with Catholic beliefs and practices at the time the

87

community is living or remembering a belief or a core event that gave rise to a practice, this approach is much more effective than an academic or catechism approach. Besides, let's keep in mind that we are helping the catechumens prepare for initiation, that is, beginnings; we are not preparing them to receive doctorates in theology.

Q. Are there resources for liturgical catechesis, or catechesis on the Liturgy of the Word?

A. Absolutely. A wealth of resources on this topic exists. (See Bibliography and Resources, page 140.)

Q. How can I establish sessions that feature an informal, faith-sharing setting when my pastor and several members of the team want a lecture/classroom approach?

A. If everyone is open to continued dialogue, then keep reading, thinking and praying about the situation—and continue the dialogue when appropriate and when such discussion might be judged most effective. In the meantime, work within the boundaries set by your pastor and the other team members.

When we get down to it, a lecture/classroom approach will do no great harm. Many, many communities conduct their initiation process this way. The classroom approach is, however, a very limited view of the dynamic vision of the Order of Initiation. But remember, conversion (even in the area of catechetical method) is a process; it takes time.

Meanwhile, make certain that your pastor and team members "come across" the right books and articles; subscribe to *Catechumenate: A Journal of Christian Initiation*, published in the Archdiocese of Chicago by Liturgy Training Publications; ask the North American Forum on the Catechumenate to put you on the mailing list for its newsletter *Forum*; suggest that the entire team attend a Beginnings and Beyond Institute, sponsored by the North American Forum.

(See Bibliography and Resources, page 140, for other resources.)

If the catechetical approach favored by the others isn't all that you could hope for, spend your time and energies implementing other portions of the Order of Initiation. Are the liturgical rites vibrant and powerfully executed? Do you have a sound discernment process in place? Do you provide spiritual direction for your participants? How are the hospitality aspects working? Do you provide opportunities for socializing? Is your mystagogy in place and working?... Well, you get the idea.

The Order of Initiation is filled with rich possibilities, many of which have yet to be fully implemented by most communities. My friend, there is much work to be done. Don't get bogged down in catechetical method. It's certainly important, but new Christians will continue to come to the Lord and the Church in spite of our fumblings.

Q. How do you get folks to buy into an ongoing process when we all live by a nine-month (school-year, September-to-June) calendar?

A. This is very difficult. Our society as a whole is greatly influenced by the academic year. We all lived by that year for eight or twelve or sixteen years...or longer. So our deep-down-bones feeling that New Year's Day really occurs in September, that year's end is in early June, and that the summer months offer a state of blissful suspension of normal duties and responsibilities...this rhythm is pervasive in our American culture.

The first thing to do in this area of conversion is to sell your team on the idea of a year-round catechumenate that meets each Lord's Day following the sending forth of the catechumens. If you have five trained catechists and you divide the sessions up among them, each catechist would be responsible for only ten or eleven sessions during an entire year—that's less than one session each month. Now anyone can commit to a schedule like that.

If you can convince everyone that this approach makes sense and that it really won't be a burden (initially, the idea of weekly year-round meetings sounds overwhelming), you're well on your way to breaking the academic-year mind-set and "resetting" everyone's internal calendars.

The year-round catechumenate actually takes a tremendous amount of pressure off everyone. It also reforms the way everyone thinks about the process. Suddenly, you don't have to think in terms of "classes" of catechumens (as in the "class of '93"). You also don't have to worry in February about how to integrate a latecomer into a group that was formed the previous September. Folks come and go according to *their* needs, not according to when the parish is organizing the "next class."

11. Pastoral Situations

Godparents

Q. Who chooses the godparents?

A. The person to be baptized has the right under canon law (Canon 874.1) to choose her or his godparent. The choice, however, is to be approved by the priest (*RCIA*, 11, 13), who sees that the person chosen meets the qualifications of a godparent.

Q. What are the qualifications of a godparent?

A. A godparent must be:

- at least sixteen years of age (although exceptions may be made for pastoral reasons);
- a fully initiated Catholic (one who has been baptized and confirmed and has received the Eucharist);
- leading a life in harmony with the faith.

In addition, a godparent must not be:

- prohibited from serving as a godparent because of any legitimate Church penalty;
- the father or mother of the one to be baptized (Canon 874).

Q. Does the requirement that a godparent "lead a life in harmony with the faith" (Canon 874.1, 3) automatically disqualify someone who is living in an irregular marriage from serving as a godparent?

A. Not necessarily. There seems to be no clear prohibition in the law. What is important is the quality of the person's faith life. However, you must be aware that during the catechumenate, there will be difficult and uncomfortable times for such a godparent—

and for the catechumen. These times would include discussions of the Church's view of the indissolubility of marriage. The situation will also be especially painful during the rites when the catechumen celebrates sacraments that the godparent cannot fully participate in, for example, reception of Holy Communion.

Much thought, prayer and pastoral wisdom needs to be brought to any decision involving the choice of a godparent, especially if that potential godparent is living in an irregular marriage.

Q. May a good Christian who is not a Catholic serve as a godparent?

A. No. But he or she may stand as a Christian witness to baptism together with a Catholic godparent (Canon 874.2).

Q. May an elect choose a godparent of the opposite gender?

A. Yes. Under the 1917 *Code of Canon Law*, it was forbidden to have a godparent of the opposite gender as a sponsor for an adult because the lifelong spiritual relationship established between the baptized person and the godparent was seen as so close as to create an impediment to marriage—if that became a possibility.

The 1983 Code of Canon Law, however, is silent regarding the gender of the godparent in relation to the gender of the one to be baptized. It simply says that "only one male or one female sponsor[16] or one of each sex is to be employed."

Q. Is it a good idea to have a spouse, a fiancé or fiancée as one's godparent?

A. There are two schools of thought on this question. Ultimately, the answer depends on the relationship of the couple. But first, let's look at the two viewpoints.

Some people who minister in the Order believe that the spousal or engaged status of the couple provides an already established intimate relationship in which deep sharing can take place.

Others (and I find myself among these) believe that it is not good for a spouse or fiancé(e) to serve as a godparent because the catechumen may need a somewhat "disinterested" third party to talk to. This would be especially important if some of the discussion that needs to take place concerns the relationship between the catechumen and his or her spouse or fiancé(e).

In the case of an engaged couple, an additional concern is the permanency of the relationship. What happens if the couple decides not to marry? What do you do if the breakup occurs the week before Easter? A short time after Easter?

For these reasons, I generally discourage a catechumen from choosing her or his fiancé(e) as a godparent. The engaged partner should, however, be encouraged to accompany the other on the journey.

Pastoral wisdom suggests that we discuss the responsibilities and expectations of a godparent with the catechumen at an early stage—before choices have been made. During this discussion, a frank exchange should take place regarding both the positive and negative aspects of choosing a spouse or a fiancé(e) as a godparent.

Marriage Questions

Q. Let's talk about people who have been divorced and remarried and who want to join the Church. I know of one instance in which the pastor and the parish coordinator of the Order of Initiation didn't find out about a divorce and remarriage until just before the Rite of Election. It was devastating to the catechumen involved because she was not allowed to continue in the process. How do we prevent this from happening?

A. It is most important to find out about marriage situations immediately. A well-designed initial information form is essential (see Appendix: Sample Information and Interview Forms, page 121).

Q. Are divorced and remarried inquirers allowed to enter the catechumenate?

A. Yes. An unbaptized person who is divorced and remarried may be accepted into the Order of Catechumens. However, the catechumen may not celebrate the Rite of Election until she or he is free to marry in the Church.

The Rite of Election marks the fact that the person elected has been enrolled to celebrate the Sacraments of Initiation at the *next* Easter Vigil. If no decision on the person's freedom to marry has been made at the time of the Rite of Election, no presumption can or should be made that a decision in the catechumen's favor will be made before the Easter Vigil.

Q. What about candidates? May they participate in the Rite of Welcoming?

A. There is nothing in the *Ordo* that prohibits a baptized person in an irregular marriage from participating in the Rite of Welcoming. However, pastoral care must be exercised to ensure that such a public welcoming would not cause scandal within the community. If scandal is a factor, it would be better to welcome the candidate privately, with, perhaps, only the catechumenal community present.

Q. May candidates who are living in irregular marriages participate in the Call to Continuing Conversion?

A. I don't see how this would be possible.

In presenting the candidates to the bishop, the representative of the local community asks that they be admitted to Confirmation and the Eucharist "after this Lenten season," that is, at the upcoming Easter Vigil. Later in the ritual, the bishop asks the sponsors if the candidates are "ready to receive the sacraments of confirmation and the eucharist" (*RCIA*, 555, 556). If a marriage case is pending in the Church courts, no sponsor can honestly answer this question in the affirmative. By definition, the candidate is not ready.

So, candidates should be advised that they are welcome to journey with us and to associate themselves with the catechumenate if they are not catechized. However, they need to know that they cannot proceed further in the process until their marriage situation is resolved favorably.

Q. It seems very inhospitable to me to be laying all these prohibitions on these people. Isn't there an easier way?

A. As ministers in the Order of Christian Initiation of Adults, we must always proceed in these instances with much care and discernment. If, in the Order of Initiation, we are forming people to witness to the truth and to live in justice and love, then we ourselves must be clear from the beginning about our Church's belief in the indissolubility of marriage.

Through the various rites of the Order of Initiation, an individual makes a public commitment to follow Jesus Christ, to live a gospel life, to take upon herself or himself the duties and responsibilities of the Christian life. Persons in irregular marriages—precisely because of the irregularity of their marriages—are unable to witness to the teaching of Jesus and of the Church regarding the indissolubility of marriage.

We must also be conscious of and sensitive to those people in our communities who may be in similar marriage situations—some of which are impossible to resolve either because of lack of evidence that proves that the previous marriage was invalid or because their previous marriage was indeed a valid one. What effect will their seeing divorced and remarried couples entering into full communion have upon their faith life? This is an area where the utmost care and the deepest pastoral wisdom must be exercised.

Q. What do we do when a person in an irregular marriage inquires about joining the Catholic Church?

A. Welcome them and explain to them that from the Catholic Church's point of view they may be bound by the natural bond of their first marriage. Take some time to talk with them about the Church's view concerning the indissolubility of marriage and the importance our faith community places on marriage.

You should also explain briefly that, in many cases, an investigation by a Church court (tribunal) can uncover circumstances that show that no marriage may have truly existed from the Church's point of view. If that turns out to be the case, then they would be free to be admitted to the Sacraments of

Initiation or to complete their initiation.

If possible, you should then set up an appointment for the inquirer with the community's priest.

Q. Can you tell me a little about the various types of marriage situations and how the Church handles them? What kinds of situations can I expect to see?

A. This is a very complex and confusing area. Canon lawyers (like civil lawyers) spend years learning about the ins and outs, the subtleties, of the law—in the case of canon lawyers, the subtleties of Church law. However, in a very simplified form, here are the major situations that you are most likely to come across in your ministry in the Order of Initiation:

(In each of these examples, the person seeking to enter the Catholic Church is currently in a second marriage.)

Defect in Form. Mary has never been baptized and is divorced from John, a Catholic. They were married outside the Church (for example, by a justice of the peace, a judge, a Protestant minister, and so forth) without a dispensation from John's bishop. This marriage is considered by the Church to have been defective in form,[17] and, in the Church's view, was invalid (that is, no marriage took place). Therefore, Mary was free to marry her current spouse.

The only documents needed to prove this case are John's baptismal record, a copy of John and Mary's marriage application and certificate of the marriage and a copy of their divorce decree.

Pauline Privilege.[18] Dorothy is not baptized but wishes to become a Catholic Christian. She is divorced from Thomas who also is not baptized. The Pauline privilege may be invoked here. Because neither party was baptized, no sacramental marriage exists.

Privilege of the Faith. Richard is unbaptized and had been married to a baptized Christian who is not Catholic. His present spouse was not the reason for the failure of the first marriage. In fact, Richard didn't even meet his present spouse until eight months after his divorce. This is a "privilege of the faith" case. The first marriage may be dissolved by the pope.

The local tribunal processes both Pauline-privilege and privilege-of-the-faith cases, but it decides only the Pauline-privilege cases, with the pope deciding those cases involving the privilege of the faith.[19]

Prior Bond. Bill and Sue are both baptized and both wish to be received into full communion with the Catholic Church. However, Sue was previously married to Ray, but that was Ray's second marriage: he was previously married to Jane.

In the view of the Church, the bond of marriage between Ray and Jane still exists, so that Ray was not free to marry Sue. Therefore, Bill and Sue are free to marry.

This situation must be handled by the local tribunal. The tribunal would investigate the marriage of Ray and Sue to show by documents that Ray was previously married to Jane and therefore was not free to marry Sue. This process would show that Bill and Sue are free to enter and marry in the Church.

Formal Cases. Formal cases have to do with the quality of the consent given by the two parties when they entered into the marriage bond. It is the quality of consent that "makes marriage" for all the baptized. Therefore, formal cases examine the circumstances that may have influenced the quality of the consent given, and these cases ask the question whether a sacramental union ever existed.

For example, the Church believes that a person is not capable of contracting a marriage if he or she lacks:

• sufficient use of reason (mental retardation, for instance);

• judgment (because of immaturity, undue pressure, youth and other reasons);

• capacity (confusion about one's sexual orientation, the existence of some sort of psychopathology, and so forth).

A person also is not capable of contracting a marriage if he or she:

• entered into the marriage consciously intending something that is in conflict with the marriage vows (for instance, a decision not to have children);

• was forced or was in fear of her or his life or safety (the "shotgun wedding," for example).

These, then, are the major situations that you are likely to encounter in your ministry in the Order of Initiation.

Initiation of Children

Q. I noticed that the Rite of Christian Initiation of Adults has a section in it dealing with the initiation of *children*. What is this doing in a document on *adult* initiation?

A. A portion of the *Ordo*—about 160 pages and nearly 80 "paragraphs," or sections—discusses the initiation of children who have reached catechetical age. What is this section doing in a document entitled *Rite of Christian Initiation of Adults*? Well, the *Code of Canon Law* requires that "what is prescribed in the canons on the baptism of an adult is applicable to all who are no longer infants but have attained the use of reason" (Canon 852.1).

Infancy, according to Church law, comes to an end around the age of seven (Canon 97.2). So, an unbaptized child who is at least seven years old must be initiated into Catholic Christianity according to the process prescribed in the *Rite of Christian Initiation of Adults*, 252 to 330.

Q. What is involved?

A. The process outlined in the *Ordo* very much resembles the adult process.

It calls for a gradual incorporation of the child into the community over an extended period of time marked by ritual celebrations, including a Rite of Acceptance into the Order of Catechumens; an optional Rite of Election with the bishop or his delegate; Penitential Rites (Scrutinies), with the celebration of the Liturgy of Penance (Sacrament of Reconciliation) for those children who have already been baptized and are preparing for entrance into the Catholic Church; and the celebration of the

Sacraments of Initiation. A period of mystagogy is also suggested. The *Ordo* is insistent that the process meet the children where they are. This means, among other things, that special catechists should be dedicated to this ministry, parents and other relatives should be intimately involved, and the liturgies should be designed to speak to the children involved.

The North American Forum on the Catechumenate sponsors special workshops and institutes whose sole focus is the initiation of children of catechetical age. These workshops and institutes are highly recommended.

(See Bibliography and Resources, page 140, for the address and telephone number of the Forum.)

Q. I've heard that if a child is baptized according to this process, the child must also be confirmed at the same time. Is this true?

A. Yes. In fact, the *Ordo* is explicit:

> At this third step of their Christian initiation, the children will receive the sacrament of baptism, the bishop or priest who baptizes them will also confer confirmation, and the children will for the first time participate in the liturgy of the eucharist. (*RCIA*, 305)

Q. Doesn't this mean that we are operating under two different systems, with some children celebrating Baptism, Confirmation and Eucharist at one ceremony and some children (those baptized before age seven) celebrating these sacraments over many years?

A. Yes. At the present moment, two or more theologies and practices are clashing. The picture becomes even more confused when you realize that various dioceses in the United States confirm those children baptized as infants at different times, ranging from age seven (prior to First Eucharist) to young adulthood, with most dioceses confirming during adolescence (ages fourteen to seventeen). The U.S. bishops are presently reevaluating this practice and will be bringing some uniformity to the situation in the near future.

12. Getting Started

Q. I've just been asked to serve as the parish coordinator of the Order of Initiation. How do I get started? Where do I begin?

A. First of all, if the Order of Initiation is being implemented for the first time in your parish, please, please, please, go *slowly*. Take your time. Think in terms of implementing the Order in stages over a number of years. Strive to do the basics well before moving on to the implementation of the next piece.

Q. What do you consider the basics?

A. The basics are, of course, what you and your parish are *capable of implementing* given your unique situation. No one can expect you to do more than you can do. On the other hand, don't be too quick to decide that such and such is just impossible to accomplish. Be practical, but be honest with yourself.

Here's what might be considered "the basics":

• Some sort of precatechumenate activity. Enough meetings (even one-on-one sessions, if you have only a few inquirers) to answer the inquirers' basic and most pressing questions and enough sessions to allow you or a member of your team to get to know a bit about the inquirers and their circumstances. You must come to know the inquirers well enough to be able to recognize the signs of initial conversion.[20] This recognition tells you and the inquirers that they are ready to take the next step—celebration of the first public liturgical ceremony of the Order of Initiation: the Rite of Acceptance or the Rite of Welcoming, as appropriate.

• Celebration of the Rite of Acceptance, the Rite of Welcoming, or both, as appropriate.

• Weekly catechumenal sessions, employing liturgical catechesis and ideally following the catechumens' dismissal from the Liturgy of the Word each Lord's Day.

• Celebration of the Rite of Election and the Call to Continuing Conversion with the bishop or his delegate.

• Celebration of at least two of the three scrutinies with the elect.[21]

• Celebration of the Sacraments of Initiation at the Easter Vigil.

• Celebration of the Neophyte Masses with the parish from the Second Sunday of Easter to Pentecost.

• Monthly mystagogy meetings for one year.

If it is impossible for you to implement these basics during the first year, you might want to contact neighboring parishes and explore with them the possibilities of putting a joint process into place. Or, if a neighboring parish is well on its way to full implementation, perhaps there are portions of its process that your parish could participate in.

While the liturgical celebrations should normally occur with the specific parish community that the catechumens and candidates are joining, many of the catechetical sessions, especially the inquiry sessions of the precatechumenate, can easily be a shared venture.

If you can do nothing else, make certain that you celebrate the rites well.

Q. So, what are the first steps?

A. The very first thing you need to do is to plan:

• Meet with your pastor or parish life coordinator[22] to determine his or her expectations of you and of the Order of Initiation (time frame, time line, what portions to implement first, level of his or her involvement, budget and so forth).

• Recruit, organize and train a core team.

• With the members of your core team, decide if you need subsidiary teams (see page 104 for discussion of establishing several teams).

• Recruit and train catechists, parish sponsors, hosts and hostesses and other ministers as needed.

• Decide how you wish to handle your precatechumenate (for instance, one-on-one meetings, welcoming households, inquiry sessions in homes, inquiry sessions on the parish grounds and so forth).

• In consultation with your pastor and/or sacramental minister[23] and the parish liturgist, establish the times and dates for the celebration of the major parish rites:

> 1) Rite of Acceptance into the Order of Catechumens and the Rite of Welcoming Candidates (at least two dates, more if you are expecting many inquirers). (See "Liturgical Rites," pages 43 to 44 and pages 58 to 59 for discussion on appropriate times for this celebration.)
>
> 2) Scrutinies (the Third, Fourth and Fifth Sundays of Lent).
>
> 3) Sacraments of Initiation (at the Easter Vigil).

• Check with your diocesan office of worship for the time and date(s) of the celebration of the Rite of Election and Call to Continuing Conversion. Also determine at that time whether your bishop celebrates a Mass of Thanksgiving with the neophytes and newly received Catholics during the Easter season. If this is done in your diocese, add that date and time to the calendar, too.

• Decide if you will establish a year-round catechumenate.

• Decide if you will dismiss the catechumens from the Lord's Day assembly for catechesis on the Liturgy of the Word or whether you will hold these sessions at another time, for example, on Wednesday evenings.

• Decide at which Mass or Masses during the Easter season the neophytes and newly received will be present to celebrate the Neophyte Masses with the community. (See Bibliography and Resources, page 140. My book *Cenacle Sessions* contains specific suggestions about involving neophytes in these special Masses.)

• Establish and publish a calendar giving the dates and times of all events: the precatechumenate sessions, the Rite of Acceptance and Rite of Welcoming, the catechumenate sessions, the Rite of Election and Call to Continuing Conversion, the Scrutinies, the Initiation Sacraments at the Easter Vigil, the Neophyte Masses of the Easter season, and the monthly mystagogy meetings.

Q. About recruitment: How do you staff the process? How do you find people with the commitment and energy that is so necessary?

A. Don't try to do it by putting a general notice in the parish bulletin asking for volunteers. Recruitment for the team should be done on a one-to-one basis. If you are a member of a very large parish and don't want to overlook anyone who would be a good team member, you might want to consider asking friends in the parish to nominate folks. You might also want to consider putting job descriptions for the various ministries of the Order in the parish bulletin or newsletter and asking parishioners to nominate anyone they know who would have the necessary gifts.

As with any recruitment process, have some idea of the time commitment involved. This will be the first question potential team members will ask; in fact, they'll probably ask about the time commitment before they ask about the specific competencies needed or the tasks that would need to be carried out.

Q. How many different people are we talking about to make up the team?

A. That depends on how you choose to organize yourselves.

In a very small parish that may only welcome one or two new members each year, the team might have a director/coordinator, the pastor and two or three parish sponsors. Each of these people would function in more than one ministry. For instance, the director/coordinator might also serve as catechist, liturgist and, later, mystagogue; the pastor might take on the additional ministries of catechist, spiritual director and liturgy resource person; the parish sponsors could also serve as companions and hosts/hostesses ("Marthas") for the entire group (see "Ministries," pages 9 to 12).

In a large parish, the Order might be implemented with a core team of five or six people whose primary responsibilities are planning and coordinating the ministries of a multitude of catechists, parish sponsors, liturgical ministers, hosts and hostesses, companions, several mystagogues and so on.

Q. Do we need more than one team?

A. Only you can answer that question. And you may not be able to formulate an accurate answer until you have experienced at least one complete cycle of the Order of Initiation. The important thing is to approach this work with calmness and patience.

Do not attempt to do everything yourself.

Do not attempt to do everything during the first cycle.

Plan, read, attend workshops, pray, garner tips from those ministering in the Order of Initiation in neighboring parishes.

Find at least one other person—someone on your own parish team or someone involved with the Order elsewhere—with whom you can spend time just talking about what you're doing and what you're dreaming.

Think about implementing the Order in terms of years, not in terms of months. Build slowly, but build well.

Be patient. Be patient. Be patient.

Now, let's think about the idea of establishing more than one team. Generally speaking, this makes a lot of sense. The proper implementation of the Order of Christian Initiation of Adults can be an overwhelming undertaking. It cannot be—and was never meant to be—implemented by one person. Remember that the *Ordo* itself cites the Second Vatican Council document *Decree on the Church's Missionary Activity* (*Ad gentes divinitus*, 14) to point out that it is *all the baptized* who are responsible for the initiation of adults (see also *RCIA*, 9).

I say, "generally speaking," because organizing yourselves into various teams doesn't make sense if you're doing it just to "involve" more people, or just because neighboring St. Philomena Parish is organized that way, or just because you've read about that approach somewhere. Most often, setting up multiple teams is appropriate in large parishes that initiate scores of individuals each year and that implement the Order of Initiation to its fullest extent. Ultimately the multiple-team approach makes sense only if it makes sense in your particular situation.

If your parish is large enough that several teams can be formed to carry out the various stages of the initiation process, how many teams should you have? How many people should be involved? Again, these decisions depend on your individual circumstances. As an example, let me sketch some possibilities for a fully developed multiple-team approach.

Caution: What follows is just an example. You will want to adapt it to your particular circumstances. It is not meant to be interpreted as an ideal way to organize your parish's approach to implementing the Order of Christian Initiation of Adults. The ideal for your parish is *what makes sense for your parish*. Take what is useful here and adapt, adapt, adapt.

Possible Organization I
Order of Christian Initiation of Adults
Multiple-Team Approach

Pastor/Parish Life Coordinator*
    Director/Coordinator of the Order of Initiation*

Precatechumenate/Inquiry Team
    Coordinator*
        Evangelists
        Catechists**
        Hosts/Hostesses**
        Companions**

Catechumenate Team
    Coordinator*
        Catechists**
        Liturgists/Musicians**
        Spiritual Director/Discerner**
        Parish Sponsors**
        Hosts/Hostesses**
        Companions**

Purification/Enlightenment Team[24]
    Coordinator*
        Catechists**
        Liturgists/Musicians**

Spiritual Director/Discerner**
Parish Sponsors**
Hosts/Hostesses**
Companions**

Mystagogy Team
Coordinator*
Mystagogue(s)
Spiritual Director/Discerner**
Liturgists/Musicians**
Hosts/Hostesses**
Companions**

*Members of the Core Team

**These roles may be filled by the same person serving on more than one team. For instance, the spiritual director/discerner role on each team may be filled by the same person.

Here is another model, a slightly different way of organizing the work:

Possible Organization II
Order of Christian Initiation of Adults
Multiple-Team Approach

Core Team
Pastor/Parish Life Coordinator
Director/Coordinator of the Order of Initiation
Coordinator of Precatechumenate Stage
Coordinator of Catechumenate Stage
Coordinator of Purification and
Enlightenment Stage
Coordinator of Mystagogy
Coordinator of Catechesis/Master Catechist
Coordinator of Initiation Rites
Spiritual Director(s)
Coordinator of Martha Ministries
(Hostesses/Hosts, Companions)
Inservice Coordinator (Training for all
ministers, including sponsors, godparents)

Precatechumenate/Inquiry Team
Coordinator
Evangelists
Catechists
Hosts/Hostesses
Companions

Catechumenate Team
Coordinator
Catechists
Liturgists/Musicians
Spiritual Director/Discerner
Parish Sponsors
Hosts/Hostesses
Companions

Purification/Enlightenment Team
Coordinator
Catechists
Liturgists/Musicians
Spiritual Director/Discerner
Parish Sponsors
Hosts/Hostesses
Companions

Mystagogy Team
Coordinator
Mystagogue(s)
Spiritual Director/Discerner
Liturgists/Musicians
Hosts/Hostesses
Companions

Here is a third way to organize your approach. This schema might be appropriate for a small parish, where one team makes sense and where each member of the team carries out multiple ministries:

Possible Organization III
Order of Christian Initiation of Adults
Small Parish

Initiation Team
Pastor/Spiritual Director/Mystagogue
Director/Coordinator/Catechist

Catechist(s)
Liturgical Musician
Hosts/Hostesses/Companions/Sponsors

Q. What are the most important qualities to look for in a director/coordinator?

A. The director/coordinator of the Order of Christian Initiation of Adults should be a person of prayer who knows how to dream, who is patient and who has exceptional organizational abilities, but who can be flexible at a moment's notice.

It is also important that this person be a talented juggler—someone who has the ability to keep all the balls in the air at the same time (and to do so with grace). A sense of humor certainly comes in handy, too.

Q. What is the continuing role of the director/coordinator of the Order of Christian Initiation of Adults? Regarding the teams? Regarding the parish as a whole?

A. Before we get into a discussion about what is the continuing role of the director/coordinator, let me point out that this ministry *should* be a *continuing* role. The ministry of director/coordinator of the Order of Initiation should only be taken on by an individual who can make at least a three-year commitment. If your parish is starting from scratch, even a three-year commitment by the director/coordinator may be too short. But that should be the minimum expectation.

Because so much needs to be done and because the Order should be implemented in phases, the need for continuity in leadership is very great. I have now been involved in one way or another in this work for a dozen years, and I still feel as if we are just beginning to get a grasp on what it is we are about. (If the truth be known, I'm not sure we will ever really "get a grasp" of this process. Each year, the many variables change: different candidates, different team members, sometimes a different pastor. But I have found that what especially changes is my own and others' understanding of the Order of Initiation, which is always unfolding before our eyes.)

Now, what is the continuing role of the primary local leader of the Order of Initiation? In general, it is to provide leadership, to plan, to coordinate, to provide training and inservice to the ministers involved in the Order, and to build those ministers into a real team. (Can we really call ourselves a *team* if we meet only when we are carrying out our ministries and never meet to evaluate what we are doing and to envision what we might do?) Of course, the best gift a director/coordinator can give her or his parish is a trained and seasoned successor and a team capable of carrying on with the new director/coordinator.

The director/coordinator will also be the one who speaks about the Order to the larger parish community. He or she needs to anticipate and seize teachable moments to help parish members understand what the Order of Initiation is all about and what role the community itself plays in the initiation process.

Q. What are the inservice opportunities for leaders of the Order of Initiation? Workshops? Forum? Resources? Retreats?

A. Inservice opportunities abound for leaders and ministers (see Bibliography and Resources, page 140).

Many dioceses now have offices to aid in implementing the Order of Christian Initiation of Adults throughout the diocese and to serve as resources to those serving in parishes. Some dioceses (my own is one) have chosen not to set up formal offices but rather to establish commissions or committees or other working groups made up of volunteers with the experience and expertise needed to serve as diocesan resources to parish leaders.

In addition, the North American Forum on the Catechumenate has been indefatigable in its guidance and sponsorship of workshops and institutes. A recent issue of *Catechumenate: A Journal of Christian Initiation* lists thirty-two separate Forum-sponsored workshops or institutes throughout the United States devoted to eleven different aspects of implementing the Order. (See Bibliography and Resources, page 149, for the Forum's address.)

13. A Model Process

Q. Could you outline a model process that would give me some idea what an entire initiation cycle in a typical parish would look like?

A. I do it with cautions and qualifications similar to those on page 105, where I discussed the multiple-team approach. I again emphasize that it is absolutely essential to envision the Order of Christian Initiation of Adults as a sacramental process at whose heart is the continuing conversion of individuals. Because of this vision of the Order, I must also continue to emphasize that each community must adapt this ideal to individual situations. Adapt. Adapt. Adapt. Make the vision your own.

Here is how the Order might unfold in a typical parish given the following assumptions:

1. There is no such thing as a "typical parish."

2. Our hypothetical parish, St. Richard, is a large community blessed with every possible gift of the Holy Spirit necessary for the full implementation of the Order of Initiation.

3. St. Richard Parish welcomes about an even mix of unbaptized and baptized inquirers.

4. The parish has been implementing the Order of Initiation using a nine-month (September to Easter) model and has decided to move to a more or less continuous inquiry series and a year-round catechumenate.

5. For simplicity's sake, the following calendar has not been constructed as a master calendar; it will track only one group of individuals,[25] most of whom will celebrate the initiation sacraments at the Easter Vigil of 1995. Another calendar, tracking the continuous inquiry sessions, follows this first calendar.

6. The following calendar is a "real calendar" in the sense that the dates and liturgical feasts and seasons are accurate for the years

given. This is done to give you a sense of "real time."

St. Richard Parish
Order of Christian Initiation of Adults
Calendar

1993
Post-Easter

Each new inquirer who has approached the parish since Easter 1993 has met for initial interviews with the director/coordinator of the Order of Initiation and the pastor. Both the director and the pastor, or parish life coordinator,[26] have been "sorting" the inquirers to determine their needs.

A few inquirers have been received into full communion with the Church during these months because they have come to us nearly ready.

Since St. Richard's year-round inquiry sessions and catechumenate have not yet begun, others—those who are not baptized and those baptized inquirers who have had little or no catechesis—have been meeting periodically with a longtime parishioner and catechist who is getting to know them, answering their questions and telling them about her own faith journey and about the local community. Once the year-round inquiry sessions and the every-Sunday catechumenal meetings begin, inquirers will no longer have to be placed on hold.

August 4 and 25

Final organizational meetings with the team and the various ministers.

September 8—December 15

Inquiry sessions are held weekly on Wednesday evenings in cycles of approximately fourteen weeks (see page , for an example of a possible inquiry schedule). No sessions meet on November 24, the evening before Thanksgiving Day.

1994

January 3—January 22

Inquirers meet individually with spiritual directors to discern their readiness to enter the next stage: the catechumenate for those not baptized; association with the catechumenate for those baptized but not catechized.

January 26—May 11

A new (second) inquiry series begins for those who arrived at our doors in November and December or who were not yet ready to join the catechumenate. (See second calendar [p. 115], which continues to track these inquiry sessions.)

January 23

Celebration of the Combined Rite of Acceptance into the Order of Catechumens and Rite of Welcoming.

Third Sunday in Ordinary Time (Cycle B): The Scripture readings assigned for this Lord's Day are Jonah 3:1-5, 10: the people of Nineveh hear God's word and repent; 1 Corinthians 7:29-31: the time is short, the world is passing away; and Mark 1:14-20: the reign of God is at hand. Repent and believe the Good News!

The new catechumens and the candidates who are joining themselves to the catechumenate are dismissed at the end of these readings and the homily, but before the Creed and General Intercessions. They process to the catechumeneon, their special meeting room, with a catechist to break open the word and to reflect on the rites they have just experienced.

January 23, 1994—February 26, 1995

The catechumenate meets each Lord's Day with the assembly for the Liturgy of the Word and is dismissed to the catechumeneon with a catechist to continue the Liturgy of the Word. (Note: 1995 is not a typographical error; this is more than one year's worth of meetings as called for by National Statute 6.)

The catechumens and candidates also meet periodically as individuals with a spiritual director. Candidates should be advised that the Sacrament of Reconciliation is available to them at any time. Catechesis on this sacrament should take place early during this period.

1995

As the time for election approaches (March 5), catechumens and candidates continue to meet with the spiritual director, the director/coordinator, the pastor, their sponsors, or others to discern their readiness to enter the next stage of the journey.

March 1: Ash Wednesday

Parish Celebration for Sending Catechumens for Election and Candidates for Recognition by the Bishop.

The catechumens and the candidates who have joined themselves to the catechumenate are dismissed at the end of these rites to break open the word and to reflect on the rites they have just experienced.

March 5: Lent I

Celebration of the Rite of Election of Catechumens and of the Call to Continuing Conversion of Candidates with the bishop at the cathedral church.

March 10-12

Sleep-at-home retreat (Friday/Saturday/Sunday) at the parish for the elect and candidates, godparents, sponsors and team members. The retreat culminates on Sunday morning with the celebration of the Penitential Rite (Scrutiny) with the candidates (see next entry).

March 12: Lent II

Celebration of the Penitential Rite with the candidates.

Following this rite, the candidates and the elect are sent forth to break open the word and to reflect on the rite just experienced and on the cathedral rites of the previous Lord's Day (if there has not yet been an opportunity to do so).

March 19: Lent III

Celebration of the First Scrutiny with the elect. The *Cycle*

A readings are proclaimed during this celebration even though this is a Cycle C year (see page 45 for discussion).

Following this rite, the elect and the candidates are dismissed to break open the word and to reflect on the rites they have just experienced.

March 26: Lent IV

Celebration of the Second Scrutiny with the elect (following the proclamation of the readings from Cycle A).

Following this rite, the elect and the candidates are dismissed to break open the word and to reflect on the rites they have just experienced.

April 2: Lent V

Celebration of the Third Scrutiny with the elect (following the proclamation of readings from Cycle A).

Following this rite, the elect and the candidates are dismissed to break open the word and to reflect on the rites they have just experienced.

April 9: Passion/Palm Sunday

Celebration of the Liturgy of the Word with the assembly, with dismissal and breaking open the word as usual.

April 15/Morning

Celebration of the Preparation Rites (see pages 56 to 57 and *Ordo*, 185ff.).

April 15/Evening, beginning in the dark, after sundown

Celebration of the Sacraments of Initiation at the Great Vigil.

April 16—June 4: Eastertide—The Great Fifty Days

Immediate mystagogy: reflection on the readings of these Eastertide Sundays and participation in the Lord's Day Eucharists of the community (see Bibliography and Resources: Mystagogy, page 147).

June 14

> First of nine or ten monthly mystagogy gatherings that
> will continue until the celebration of the next Great Vigil.

1996
April 6

> Mystagogy ends with a reception following the Great
> Vigil.

Here is a second calendar that tracks the inquiry sessions that will
be taking place during 1994 and 1995. (Please note that while
these inquiry sessions are taking place, the catechumens will be
meeting every Sunday, and, after Eastertide, the neophytes will be
meeting monthly.)

> **St. Richard Parish**
> **Order of Christian Initiation of Adults**
> **Inquiry Sessions Calendar**

1994
January 26

> A new (second) inquiry series begins for those who
> arrived at our doors in November and December or who
> were not yet ready to join the catechumenate. It continues
> until May 11.

May 12—June 11

> Inquirers meet individually with spiritual directors to
> discern their readiness to enter the next stage.

May 18

> New (third) inquiry series begins; it will continue until
> August 17.

June 12

> Celebration of the Combined Rite of Acceptance into the
> Order of Catechumens and Rite of Welcoming.
>
> Eleventh Sunday in Ordinary Time (Cycle B). Scripture
> readings: The Lord has made a small tree (Israel) great;

we walk by faith and not by sight; the parable of the mustard seed.

July 20—August 20

Inquirers meet individually with spiritual directors to discern their readiness to enter the next stage.

August 21

Celebration of the Combined Rite of Acceptance into the Order of Catechumens and Rite of Welcoming.

Twenty-First Sunday in Ordinary Time (Cycle B). The Scriptures speak of the renewal of the covenant by Joshua and the people, the marriage of Christ to his Church and Simon Peter's declaration: "We have come to believe; we are convinced that you are God's holy one."

September 7

New (fourth) inquiry series begins; it continues until December 14.

December 15—January 13

Inquirers meet individually with spiritual directors to discern their readiness to enter the next stage.

1995

January 22

Celebration of the Combined Rite of Acceptance into the Order of Catechumens and of the Rite of Welcoming.

Third Sunday in Ordinary Time (Cycle C). The Scriptures speak of Israel's commitment to the Torah, the different roles of the members of the Body of Christ and the inauguration of Jesus' ministry.

February 1

New (fifth) inquiry series begins; it will continue until May 24.

May 25—June 23

Inquirers meet individually with spiritual directors to discern their readiness to enter the next stage.

Celebration of the Combined Rite of Acceptance into the Order of Catechumens and of the Rite of Welcoming.

Twelfth Sunday in Ordinary Time (Cycle C). The Scripture readings deal with Zechariah's prophecy of the suffering Messiah, the fact that all Christians are one in Christ Jesus and Peter's profession of faith in Jesus as the Messiah of God.

And so the cycles continue.

14. Discernment

Q. What is discernment?

A. Thomas Morris points out in his book *The RCIA: Transforming the Church* that discernment, at least as it's used in the Order of Initiation, is about making choices in life. These choices generally deal with choosing between two good things (rather than choosing between good and evil or good and bad).

Discernment is a method of sorting through two or more options or directions in life and, through prayer, study, reflection and the input of others, making a good decision. In doing this, the person recognizes that God is still pursuing a passionate love affair not only with all creation and all people as a community, but also with each individual. God loves each of us, and it is God's will that we be happy.

The Order of Initiation contains two major decision points: whether to enter the catechumenate and whether to be baptized. The ultimate decision to become a catechumen generally rests with the inquirer; the ultimate decision about Baptism rests with the Church in the person of its chief pastor, the bishop, through the local pastor.

Inquirers who are already baptized but have not received catechesis will be going through similar decision-making points, although their one major decision is whether to make a profession of faith and enter into full communion with the Catholic Church.

Q. Why should we be deciding (or discerning) whether an individual is "ready" for Baptism or whatever? Isn't this the proper role of the Holy Spirit?

A. Yes. These are certainly decisions that we place under the inspiration of the Holy Spirit. But Catholic belief holds that the movement, the action, of God in our lives normally occurs through ordinary people and events; it does not normally come through instant flashes of understanding or voices or visions. So, it is a constitutive part of our role as ministers in the Order of Initiation to assist inquirers and catechumens in listening to what the Spirit is saying to them.

Also integral to the Church's understanding of ministry is what I call, for lack of a better image, the "echo effect." As a community of faith, we believe that individuals are called to God, to the community and to service within that community. We also believe, however, that God's call must be "echoed," affirmed or confirmed, by the community, which is itself Spirit-filled and Spirit-led.

So, decisions about membership and service in the Church are not merely an individual's decision; they must be a decision arrived at jointly by an individual and by the community, both of whom rely on the inspiration and guidance of the Holy Spirit.

Q. Under what circumstances would you refuse to allow a person to continue to the next step in the Order of Initiation?

A. I can think of only a few instances when this might be necessary. Occasionally, a person has to be "put on hold" while a marriage irregularity is being worked out through the Church courts.

These marriage situations aside, circumstances that necessitate a refusal to accept someone as a catechumen or as an elect are very few and far between. Two instances would be continued evidence that conversion in the area of life and morals has not taken place in the inquirer and any obvious coercion of the person by family, in-laws or others.

Q. How do you determine that a person is ready to move to the next step?

A. These decisions should always be made in the context of dialogue (with the person, sponsors, team members), prayer and community.

The *Ordo* sets forth benchmarks to help us in the discernment process (*RCIA*, 42). The decision to move from inquirer status to that of catechumen should be based upon evidence showing:

- the beginnings of the growth of spiritual life and the understanding of the fundamentals of Christian teaching;

- initial faith and conversion;

- an intention to change their lives and to enter into a relationship with God in Christ;

- the first stirrings of repentance;

- the beginnings of prayer by the person;

- a sense of the Church within the person;

- some experience by the person of the company and spirit of Christians through contact with Christians.

The *Ordo* points out that "[b]efore the rite of election the bishop, priests, deacons, catechists, godparents, and the entire community, in accord with their respective responsibilities and in their own way, should, after considering the matter carefully, arrive at a judgment about the catechumens' state of formation and progress" (*RCIA*, 121).

And how should all these ministers arrive at that judgment? Again, according to the *Ordo*, the decision to move from the status of catechumen to that of elect should be based upon evidence showing:

- a conversion in mind and in action;

- a sufficient acquaintance with Christian teaching;

- a sufficient acquaintance with the spirit of faith and charity;

- the intention to receive the sacraments of the Church, arrived at with "deliberate will and an enlightened faith" (*RCIA*, 119, 120).

Appendix:
Sample Information and Interview Forms

General Information Form

Name _____

Street _____

City, state, ZIP _____

Place of employment _____

Telephone _____

Home _____

Work _____

Date of birth _____

Place of birth _____

Father's name _____

Father's religion _____

Mother's maiden name _____

Mother's religion _____

Have you ever been baptized? _____

If so, when and where?

Date of Baptism _____

Name of Church _____

City _____

Name of minister _____

Marital Status

____ Never married
____ Married only once
____ Presently married
____ Presently separated
____ Divorced not remarried
____ Divorced and remarried

Spouse's name _____

Has your spouse ever been baptized? _____

If so, when and where?

Date of Baptism _____

Name of Church _____

City _____

Name of minister _____

Were you married in a Catholic Church? _____

If so, when and where?_____

_____

Name of priest _____

Were you married in another Church? _____

If so, when and where?_____

_____

Name of minister _____

Were you married by a justice of the peace, a judge, other? _____

If so, when and where?_____

_____

Name of person performing the ceremony _____

Other information

Please list the names of other family members (spouse, children, brothers, sisters, others).

_____

_____

_____

_____

_____

_____

_____

_____

_____

Which one of these statements best describes why you are here:

_____ I want to know more about Christianity.

_____ I'm just curious about Catholics.

_____ I want to know more about the Catholic Church.

_____ I think I want to become a Catholic.

_____ I'm pretty sure I want to become a Catholic.

_____ I know that I want to become a Catholic.

What is the best day and time of the week for you to meet with us?

_____

_____

The First Interview

Name _____

Date _____

Tell me about your experiences of God.

Where did you learn about God?

[If the person is baptized]
What meaning did your Baptism have for you?

What role has religion/the Church played in your life?

Why are you interested in the Catholic Church?

Do you know anyone who is Catholic? Family members? Friends? Coworkers?

Do you know anyone here at St. Richard Parish?

Do you have any specific questions I can try to answer for you right now?

How much time are you willing to invest in this search you're on?

[Briefly explain the Order of Christian Initiation of Adults as it is being implemented at St. Richard; include time frames, time commitments, other expectations.]

Other information

Notes

[1] Tertullian, the great father of the Church from Carthage, wrote the *Apology* (*Apologeticum*) about A.D. 197. In this work, he makes the statement: "Persons are not born Christians, but become such." Tertullian wanted to assure his pagan readers that Christians are ordinary humans who have come to belief in God, Jesus and resurrection from the dead. The fact that Christians are made and not born is critical to our understanding of what we are about as members of the Church and as ministers in the Order of Christian Initiation.

[2] "The initiation of catechumens is a gradual process that takes place within the community of the faithful. By joining the catechumens in reflecting on the value of the paschal mystery and by renewing their own conversion, the faithful provide an example that will help the catechumens to obey the Holy Spirit more generously." (*Rite of Christian Initiation of Adults, Ordo initiationis christianae adultorum* [*RCIA*], 4)

[3] Michael's Confirmation is reserved to the local bishop. Canon 883.2 and National Statutes 28 and 29 are clear that priests with an office of pastoral care (pastor, parochial vicar, chaplain and others) have the faculty to confirm already baptized *Catholics* when they are being received back into the Church. This would occur when the person involved is (1) a baptized Catholic who has apostatized, (2) a baptized Catholic who has been instructed in or has joined a non-Catholic religion through no fault of his or her own.

However, the local priest does not have the faculty to confirm a Catholic who through no fault of his or her own has never put the faith into practice. These Catholics have never actually "left" the Church and therefore they cannot be received back into it.

In Michael's case, even if he has practiced the faith, his "Catholic connection" through Baptism ties him to the local bishop for Confirmation. If the local priest wishes to confirm Michael, he must request that faculty from the bishop.

[4] Matthew, also baptized in the Catholic Church, may be confirmed by the local priest because he joined another Christian Church because of the action of his parents (see case 2 in note 3).

[5] Lucia's Confirmation is reserved to the bishop (see case 1 in note 3). Again, if a local priest holding a pastoral office wishes to confirm Lucia, he must request this faculty from the bishop.

[6] The catechumeneon is the place where the catechumens regularly meet. In most parishes, this will be a multipurpose room of some sort. Let us pray for the day when, in the construction of new churches or in their renovation, we will see specific areas designed for adults and their learning/worshiping needs.

[7] It seems that these are words that Hilaire Belloc might or should have said. My search to find the name of the poem that contains this verse has been in vain. Two recent books (*How To Save the Catholic Church* by Andrew M. Greeley and Mary Greeley Durkin, p. 62, and *Why Be Catholic?* by Richard Rohr and Joseph Martos, p. 6) use the quote (slightly different in each case) to make the point that the Catholic vision of life is a vision that sees God in all of God's creation—a creation that is good.

As far as I have been able to determine, the closest Belloc gets to these words is found in his poem "Heretics All," where he says: "But Catholic men that live upon wine/Are deep in the water, and frank, and fine;/Wherever I travel I find it so,/Benedicamus Domino." Now this will hardly do to bolster a point about the Catholic understanding of pervasive sacramentality. But the idea is great. So if Belloc didn't say it, perhaps he should have!

[8] Regarding baptized and uncatechized adults, the *Ordo* reminds us that "[e]ven though uncatechized adults have not yet heard the message of the mystery of Christ, their status differs from that of catechumens, since by Baptism they have already become members of the Church and children of God" (*RCIA*, 400).

For those who have been baptized, catechized and active in another Church community, the *Ordo* emphasizes that "[a]nything that would equate candidates for reception with those who are catechumens is to be absolutely avoided" (*RCIA*, 477).

The National Statutes point out that "[i]t is preferable that reception into full communion not take place at the Easter Vigil lest there be any confusion of such baptized Christians with the candidates for Baptism, possible misunderstanding of or even reflection upon the Sacrament of Baptism celebrated in another Church or ecclesial community, or any perceived triumphalism in the liturgical welcome into the Catholic eucharistic community"

(*National Statutes*, 33).
And in the next statute, the U.S. bishops state: "A clear distinction should be maintained during the celebration [of the combined rite] between candidates for sacramental initiation and candidates for reception into full communion, and ecumenical sensitivities should be carefully respected" (*National Statutes*, 34).

[9] Since candidates are already baptized, it is obviously inappropriate to celebrate the exorcism/renunciation of false worship and the giving of a new name. However, many local communities like to present their catechumens with wooden crosses to mark their new identity within the community and to concretize the signing-with-the-cross ritual action that occurs within the Rite of Acceptance.

In order not to "discriminate" against baptized candidates who participate in a combined Rite of Acceptance and Welcoming, these communities also present the candidates with a cross.

In the Rite of Acceptance, the marking of the senses of the unbaptized with the sign of the cross is a first marking and a first acceptance by them to "take up the cross and follow" Jesus. The marking of the baptized candidates with the sign of the cross is done in memory of their baptismal commitment.

If you believe that in presenting crosses to catechumens you must also present crosses to the candidates, you may wish to use different words for the presentation to each group. For example, the words accompanying the presentation to candidates should emphasize that the cross is a reminder of their earlier commitment to take up the cross at their baptisms.

It is important that the distinction between the baptized and the unbaptized be maintained. This is especially challenging when you celebrate combined rites. The importance of maintaining the distinction—of honoring and respecting the Baptism of the candidates—calls upon your creativity and your liturgical finesse. Many liturgists have concluded that, in this particular rite, the action of signing the senses, if the fullness of the sign is employed, speaks powerfully and is not necessarily enhanced with the additional and, in their view and mine, the superfluous presentation of a cross.

[10] Option C is used if the catechumens remain while the assembly celebrates Eucharist. Option D is used to dismiss the entire assembly in the case where no Liturgy of the Eucharist follows.

[11] While I am quite aware that I am describing a dismissal by the

presider at a Lord's Day Eucharist, where the presider must be a presbyter or bishop, I am also very much aware that in many places throughout the United States and Canada, deacons and nonordained pastoral leaders are presiding at Lord's Day communion services in the absence of a presbyter. In these communities, it is very possible that the presider at a Lord's Day communion service is a laywoman or vowed religious woman—hence my use of the pronouns *his* or *her*.

12 The Greek word here is *presbyteroi*, which means "elders." But, over the centuries, we have extended our understanding of this term to include the concept of priest. Should this expanded meaning continue in today's Church? This is an especially important question in light of our understanding of the role of the contemporary presbyter and of our restoration of the concept of each baptized believer being a priest of the New Covenant.

13 The concepts that appear in these questions regarding working with adults have been clearly articulated for the last twenty years by educators like Leon McKenzie, D.Ed., of Indiana University, whose work has had a profound effect on the way I minister with adults. Dr. McKenzie's books, especially the three listed in Bibliography and Resources, on page 141, are highly recommended. Catechists who minister to adults are indebted to Dr. McKenzie for his work in this area.

14 For further discussion of the relationship between the Gospels and the first readings in the Roman lectionary, see "Forming Catechumens Through the Lectionary," by Gerard S. Sloyan. It is found in *Before and After Baptism: The Work of Teachers and Catechists*, James A. Wilde, editor. Chicago: Liturgy Training Publications, 1988.

15 Maureen Kelly, "The Power of the Word: A Lectionary-Based Catechesis," *Breaking Open the Word of God, Cycle C*, edited by Karen Hinman Powell and Joseph P. Sinwell. Mahwah, N.J.: Paulist Press, 1988, pp. 3-5. A similar schedule is suggested by Karen Hinman Powell in "The Lectionary as a Source Book for Catechesis in the Catechumenate," *Breaking Open the Word of God: Cycle A* and *Breaking Open the Word of God: Cycle B* (see Bibliography and Resources).

16 Canon 873. Actually, the Latin literally says: "One godfather (*patrinus*) or one godmother (*matrina*) or one of each is to be

employed." The choice of the word *sponsor* to translate *patrinus* and *matrina* is unfortunate since, in the Order of Initiation, a distinction is made between godparents (baptismal sponsors) and sponsors (Confirmation sponsors or, prior to election, parish sponsors).

[17] Canon 1108. The "Catholic form" requires that the marriage take place before two witnesses and a Catholic priest, deacon, or, with permission of the Holy See, a layperson specifically delegated by the bishop.

[18] It is called Pauline because it is based on St. Paul's advice in 1 Corinthians 7:15—[If a Christian is married to a non-Christian and] "if the unbeliever wishes to separate,...let him do so. The believing husband or wife is not bound in such cases. God has called you to live in peace."

[19] Technically, both these types of cases involve "privileges of the faith." The first, which involves two unbaptized persons (one of whom wishes to convert) has traditionally been called the Pauline privilege (see note 18); the other involves one baptized and one unbaptized person who wishes to convert. Because this case is reserved to the pope, it is sometimes referred to as the Petrine privilege.

[20] The *Ordo* says that the "prerequisite for making this first step [acceptance into the Order of Catechumens] is that the beginnings of the spiritual life and the fundamentals of Christian teaching have taken root in the candidates.... [T]here must be evidence of the first faith...and of an initial conversion and intention to change their lives and to enter into a relationship with God in Christ...evidence of the first stirrings of repentance, a start to the practice of...prayer, a sense of the Church, and some experience of the company and spirit of Christians through contact with a priest or with members of the community" (*RCIA*, 42).

[21] A dispensation from your bishop is necessary if you do not celebrate all three Scrutinies (*RCIA*, 20, 34.3, 331). Since the Scrutinies are essentially identical in structure, if you are able to celebrate the required two, there is little reason not to celebrate all three. The *Ordo* envisions the inability to celebrate all three Scrutinies to lie more often than not with the elect, as in the case of serious illness.

22 Parish life coordinator is a title that is coming into general use throughout the United States to designate a person who has been given overall pastoral care of a parish by the diocesan bishop, but who is not an ordained priest. The parish life coordinator serves under a parish moderator who is an ordained priest but who is not involved in the day-to-day pastoral care of the parish. Since the terminology is still evolving, a parish life coordinator is known in some places as a parish administrator or pastoral administrator.

23 Sacramental minister represents terminology coming into general use to designate an ordained priest assigned part-time to preside at the sacramental celebrations of a parish or mission that has no resident ordained priest.

24 This group could be envisioned as a "retreat team" whose primary purpose is to make certain that the entire purification and enlightenment period (Lent) is, in fact, an extended retreat experience for the elect and their godparents, the candidates and their sponsors and the parish in general.

25 This is not meant to imply that St. Richard Parish will deal with potential new members in "classes," e.g., the catechumenal class of 1995. We may assume that some of the seekers who gather during the first inquiry series (September 8-December 15, 1993) will be baptized or received at the Easter Vigil of 1995. However, we must also assume that some won't. Some may decide early in the process not to continue; some may wish to take even more time. Again, the image here is that of a moving sidewalk at a large, modern airport. The sidewalk moves all the time; people get on and off as they need to. In this hypothetical calendar, at the 1995 Easter Vigil, we may witness the Baptism of Mary, who began her journey on September 8, 1993; and we may also see the Baptism of John, who attended his first inquiry session on January 26, 1994; in addition, Kristin, who first knocked on St. Richard's door in August 1994, might be received into full communion at the same Easter Vigil.

26 The following terms are being used more or less interchangeably to mean those persons who are not ordained priests but who have overall pastoral responsibilities for a parish community: parish life coordinator, pastoral life coordinator, parish administrator, pastoral administrator, et al.

Glossary

The Catholic Church uses a lot of strange words. Part of the reason for this is that the Church is two thousand years old and many of its words have come down to us from ancient times and ancient languages. The *Rite of Christian Initiation of Adults* naturally contains many of these terms because it is a restoration of a Church practice that dates to the first several centuries of the Church's existence.

Some people have suggested that the use of these strange words (*mystagogy* seems to be the word that is most criticized) puts people off and confuses everyone. While this may be so, on the other hand, these words carry part of our heritage—they capture something of the feeling of the tradition. And, in my mind, this reason alone is sufficient to keep—and use—these words.

Besides, no one, including the critics, has managed to come up with workable synonyms; modern English words just cannot capture the depth of meaning and the richness of history that these ancient words hold. For instance, *postbaptismal formation and integration* doesn't carry the links to our history that the single word *mystagogy* does.

So, here is a glossary of most of the "strange words" you will find in the *Rite of Christian Initiation of Adults*. Where appropriate, I have included a simple pronunciation guide and the etymology of each word, that is, the root word or words upon which our English word is based.

Words appearing in the definitions in boldface are also included as separate entries in this glossary.

candidate

A person who is a potential member of the Church. The **Ordo** uses this term generically to mean inquirers who are candidates for the **catechumenate**, **catechumens** who are candidates for election, **elect** who are candidates for Baptism, baptized seekers who are candidates for full communion with the Catholic Church, and unconfirmed Catholics who are candidates for Confirmation.

However, in the United States, those who minister in the Order of Initiation generally reserve the use of this word to mean those who have been baptized and who are seeking full communion with the Catholic Church (so they are candidates for Confirmation, Eucharist and full communion) and for those Catholics who are completing their initiation and, as such, are candidates for Confirmation and Eucharist or for Confirmation alone.

In this book, if I speak of catechumens and candidates, I'm using the two terms to differentiate unbaptized persons (catechumens) and baptized persons (candidates).

From Latin: *candidatus*, a person clothed in a white toga; from *candidus*, white.

catechist (KAT-a-kist)

A person who instructs others in the Christian faith. An ancient office in the Church that dates to apostolic times. St. Paul speaks of teaching as one of the gifts of the Holy Spirit. In most **local Churches**, catechists are blessed by the parish or the diocese to function in this ministry. Catechists are often required to meet certain standards of faith life and academic training.

From Greek: *kate-*, thoroughly; and *echein*, to sound or echo. (A catechist is to echo thoroughly the Good News of Jesus Christ in her or his life and ministry.)

catechumen (kat-a-KYEW-men)

An unbaptized person, usually an adult, who is undergoing a period of formation in the Christian faith prior to being baptized. Catechumens are considered to be members of the Church, though not yet fully initiated members. They are said to be of the "household of the faith." Canon law (Church law) sets forth certain rights and privileges for catechumens (for example, catechumens have the right to a Christian burial).

catechumenate (kat-a-KYEW-men-ate)

> The formation period before Baptism and admission into the Catholic Church. Also, the group of persons undergoing formation as Christians.

catechumeneon (kat-a-kyew-meh-KNEE-on)

> The room or place where catechumens regularly meet.

convert (KON-vert)

> A term used only of unbaptized persons who are converting to the Lord, that is, **catechumens**. While we are all undergoing continual conversion, this word should be reserved to refer to the radical conversion to Christianity. Baptized **candidates** seeking full communion should never be referred to as converts.
>
> From Latin: *convertere*, to turn around, to transform.

creed/credo (kreed/KRAY-doe)

> A summary statement of belief. The creed recited during Mass is usually the Nicene-Constantinople Creed, which was first formulated at the Council of Constantiopolitan in A.D. 381. It is an expanded version of the original Nicene Creed from the Council of Nicea in A.D. 325.
>
> Creeds became necessary when members of the Church began disagreeing on various points of belief. Creeds were an attempt by the Church to formulate written statements that would express a unity of belief. Other creeds are the Apostles' Creed and the Athanasian Creed, among many others. The creed is sometimes called the *credo*, which is Latin for *I believe*.
>
> In the ancient Church, a creed, a summary statement of belief, was called a *symbolum*, that is, a token or reminder of the faith. (The Latin word *symbolum* means *reminder* in the sense that a symbol signifies or stands for something else: It reminds one of some other thing or it evokes the memory of

something in one's mind.) Hence, in the Order of Initiation, one sometimes hears the optional rites of the Presentation of the Creed called the *Traditio Symboli* and Recitation of the Creed referred to as the *Redditio Symboli*. *Traditio* means the *handing over* or *handing on*; *redditio* means the *rendering*, *returning* or *giving back*.

Latin: *credo*, I believe; from *cor*, heart and *dare*, to give; thus, *cor dare*, to give one's heart to.

deputed (deh-PEWT-ed)

Authorized by another to act, delegated. In the Old West, ordinary citizens were deputized, or deputed, by the local sheriff to assist him. In the Order of Initiation, a deputed **catechist** is one who is authorized by the bishop to give blessings and to perform minor **exorcisms**.

Latin: *deputare*, to allot.

elect (ee-LEKT)

A **catechumen** chosen by God through the community of faith to take part in the next celebration of the Sacraments of Initiation (Baptism, Confirmation, Eucharist).

From Latin: *electio*, a choice.

election (ee-LEK-shun)

The act of choosing or being chosen. A **catechumen** is "elected" by the Lord through the Church for admission to the sacraments; this act is publicly solemnized during the Rite of Election, which usually is presided over by the bishop and celebrated on the First Sunday of Lent. Catechumens generally show their response to this act of being chosen by entering their signatures in the Book of the Elect. This is called the **enrollment** or inscription.

From Latin: *electio*, a choice.

enlightenment (en-LYE-ten-ment)

The time in the initiation process between **election** and Baptism or reception into full communion. The full name of this period in the Order of Initiation is the Period of Purification and Enlightenment. This period is meant to be a time of intense prayer, penance and preparation of the **elect** prior to the reception of the initiation sacraments. It usually coincides with the liturgical season of Lent.

enrollment

The rite or ceremony that marks the choosing of the **catechumen** for the next celebration of the initiation sacraments. Also called the inscription or **election**.

exorcism (EK-sore-siz-em)

A prayer for deliverance from evil. In the Order of Initiation, major and minor exorcisms are used to help **catechumens** in their struggle to be faithful to their new way of life. Major exorcisms tend to be more intense and forceful than the minor exorcisms.

Historically, the Church has believed catechumens to be especially vulnerable to the influence of evil and the Evil One. An anointing with the Oil of Catechumens is often part of the ritual action of exorcism. According to the *Ordo*, the major exorcisms draw the attention of the catechumens to the real nature of Christian life, the struggle between flesh and spirit, the importance of self-denial, and the need for the help of God in our daily lives (*RCIA*, 90).

From Greek: *exorkizein*, from *ex-*, away and *horkos*, oath; thus, to drive away by using an oath.

fully initiated Catholic

A person who has celebrated the three Sacraments of Initiation: Baptism, Confirmation and Eucharist.

godparent

The person who stands as an official witness of the Church to the Baptism of another. The godparent and godchild have a lifelong spiritual relationship.

inquirers

Persons seeking information about the Catholic Church. They may be baptized or unbaptized. After making a decision to enter into full communion with the Church, baptized inquirers are called **candidates**; after deciding to continue their journey toward the Easter sacraments and after celebrating the Rite of Acceptance into the Order of Catechumens, unbaptized inquirers are called **catechumens**.

lectionary (LEK-shah-nair-ee)

The book containing the readings from Scripture for use in the celebration of the liturgy. It differs from a Bible in that the readings are not continuous, but are selections arranged according to the Church year. It differs from an evangelary in that the evangelary contains only the Gospel readings and not the readings from the Hebrew Scriptures, the lesson (epistle or other reading from the Christian Scriptures) or the psalm. Because Catholics believe that the Lord is present in the word, special marks of reverence are shown to the lectionary.

From Latin: *lectionarium, legere*, to read.

local Church

A diocese or archdiocese. Also called **particular Church**. Thus, the Archdiocese of Indianapolis can also be called the Church of Indianapolis, or the local Church. The five Churches of Indiana (the Archdiocese of Indianapolis and the Dioceses of Fort Wayne-South Bend, Lafayette-in-Indiana, Evansville and Gary) can be called the local Churches of Indiana, or the particular Churches located in the state of Indiana.

mystagogy (MIS-tah-go-jee)

The period of time following Baptism during which the newly baptized spend time with the Church reflecting upon the paschal mystery and savoring their sacramental experiences. In the United States, mystagogy lasts for one year. It is also called *mystagogia* (MIS-tah-go-jee-ah). From Greek: *mystes*, an initiate; and *agein*, to lead.

mystagogue (MIS-tah-gahg)

A **catechist** who specializes in postbaptismal catechesis. The mystagogue guides the reflection of the **neophytes** during the year after their baptisms.

neophyte (NEE-ah-fight)

A recently baptized person. From Greek: *neos*, new; and *phutos*, grown: *neophutos*, newly planted, seedling.

Neophyte Masses

The Sunday Masses of the Lord's Day during Eastertide (not the Mass of Thanksgiving with the bishop). These special Masses are considered the immediate **mystagogy** for the **neophytes** and are to be followed by a year of at least monthly meetings aimed at integrating the new members fully into their communities of faith.

particular Church

A diocese or archdiocese. Also called the **local Church**.

pericope (peh-RICK-ah-pea)

A passage from a book; in our usage a passage from the

Bible officially chosen for public reading in the liturgy.
From Greek: *peri-* = around + *kope* = a cutting.

RCIA

An initialization for **R**ite of **C**hristian **I**nitiation of **A**dults (see pages 3 and 4).

rite

The manner and form of a religious ceremony. Rituals.
From Latin: *ritus*, religious custom, usage, ceremony.

sponsor

A person who accompanies someone who is seeking entry into the Church. In the Order of Christian Initiation of Adults, a sponsor stands with the **candidate** at the rites of admission to the **catechumenate** and remains as a companion and guide until the Rite of **Election**; sponsors are not the same as **godparents**, but the sponsors could serve in that capacity, too.

Bibliography and Resources

Entries marked with an asterisk (*) are highly recommended—even essential—for those readers new to ministry in the Order of Christian Initiation of Adults.

The Order of Christian Initiation, General

Catechumenate: A Journal of Christian Initiation. Chicago: Liturgy Training Publications, published six times a year.

*Dunning, James B. *New Wine: New Wineskins.* Chicago: William H. Sadlier, Inc., 1981.

Duffy, Regis A., O.F.M. *On Becoming a Catholic Christian: The Challenge of Christian Initiation.* San Francisco: Harper & Row, 1984.

Forum. Newsletter of the North American Forum on the Catechumenate. Washington, D.C.

Kemp, Raymond B. *A Journey in Faith.* New York: William H. Sadlier, Inc., 1979.

Lewinski, Ronald J. *Welcoming the New Catholic.* Revised Edition. Chicago: Liturgy Training Publications, 1983.

*Morris, Thomas H. *The RCIA: Transforming the Church.* Mahwah, N.J.: Paulist Press, 1989.

Reedy, William J., editor. *Becoming a Catholic Christian.* New York: William H. Sadlier, Inc., 1978.

Wilde, James A., editor. *Commentaries: Rite of Christian Initiation of Adults.* Chicago: Liturgy Training Publications, 1988

Adult Religious Development, Learning

Fowler, James W. *Becoming Adult, Becoming Christian: Adult Development and Christian Faith.* San Francisco: HarperSanFrancisco, 1984.

_____. *Stages of Faith: The Psychology of Human Development and the Quest for Meaning.* San Francisco: HarperSanFrancisco, 1981.

Gilligan, Carol. *In a Different Voice.* Cambridge: Harvard University Press, 1982.

Knowles, Malcolm S. *The Modern Practice of Adult Education: Androgogy Versus Pedagogy.* New York: Association Press, 1975.

Kowaski, Anita H. "Facilitating Adult Learning in the Catechumenate," *Catechumenate: A Journal of Christian Initiation.* Vol. 12, No. 2, March 1990. Chicago: Liturgy Training Publications.

McKenzie, Leon. *Adult Education and Worldview Construction.* Malabar, Fla.: Krieger Publishing Co., 1991.

_____. *Adult Religious Education: The 20th Century Challenge.* Mystic, Conn.: Twenty-Third Publications, 1975.

*_____. *The Religious Education of Adults.* Birmingham: Religious Education Press, 1982.

Robinson, Russell D. *An Introduction to Helping Adults Learn and Change.* Milwaukee: Omnibook Co., 1979.

Whitehead, Evelyn Eaton, and James D. Whitehead. *Christian Life Patterns: The Psychological Challenges and Religious Invitations of Adult Life.* New York: Doubleday, 1979.

_____. *Community of Faith: Models and Strategies for Developing Christian Communities.* Minneapolis: The Winston-Seabury Press, 1982.

_____. *Seasons of Strength: New Visions of Adult Christian Maturing.* New York: Doubleday, 1984.

Canon Law

"Divorced and Remarried Persons: Catechumenate and Sacraments," (S.C. Doct. Fid., 11 July 1983) Private. *Canon Law Digest*, Volume 10, pp. 139-140.

Huels, John M., O.S.M., J.C.D. *The Pastoral Companion: A Canon Law Handbook for Catholic Ministry.* Chicago: The Franciscan Herald Press, 1986.

Provost, James H., "Reception of Baptized Non-Catholics Who Are Divorced and Remarried," *Code, Community, Ministry: Selected Studies for the Parish Minister Introducing the Revised Code of Canon Law*. Second Edition. E. Pfnausch, editor. Washington, D.C.: Canon Law Society of America and The Catholic University of America, 1983, pp. 117-119.

"Reception/Initiation of Non-Catholics in Irregular Marriages," *Roman Replies and CLSA Advisory Opinions*, Washington, D.C.: Canon Law Society of America, 1990, pp. 95-97.

Rehrauer, Ann, O.S.F. "Welcome In! Canonical Issues and the RCIA," *CLSA Proceedings*, Washington, D.C.: Canon Law Society of America, 1990, pp. 161-169.

Catechesis, General

Bausch, William J. *Storytelling: Imagination and Faith*. Mystic, Conn.: Twenty-Third Publications, 1984.

Bokenkotter, Thomas. *Essential Catholicism*. New York: Doubleday, 1986.

DeSiano, Frank P., C.S.P. *Presenting the Catholic Faith: A Modern Catechism for Inquirers*. Mahwah, N.J.: Paulist Press, 1987.

*Foley, Leonard, O.F.M. *Believing in Jesus: A Popular Overview of the Catholic Faith*. Cincinnati: St. Anthony Messenger Press, 1981.

Hellwig, Monika K. *Understanding Catholicism*. Mahwah, N.J.: Paulist Press, 1981.

McBrien, Richard P. *Catholicism*. San Francisco: HarperSanFrancisco, 1980.

Sinwell, Joseph P. *Come Follow Me: Resources for the Period of Inquiry in the RCIA*. Mahwah, N.J.: Paulist Press, 1990.

Catechesis, Liturgical/Scriptural

*Albertus, Karen. *'Come and See': An RCIA Process Based on the Complete Lectionary Using Catholic Updates*. Leader Edition and Participant Edition. Cincinnati: St. Anthony Messenger Press, 1993.

At Home with the Word. Chicago: Liturgy Training Publications, published annually.

*Hinman, Karen, and Joseph P. Sinwell, editors. *Breaking Open the Word of God: Resources for Using the Lectionary for Catechesis in the RCIA, Cycle A.* Mahwah, N.J.: Paulist Press, 1986.

Kennedy, Dennis, C.M. "The Lectionary as Content," *The Chicago Catechumenate*, Volume 8, Number 3, March 1986, pp. 13-17.

*Powell, Karen Hinman, and Joseph P. Sinwell, editors. *Breaking Open the Word of God: Resources for Using the Lectionary for Catechesis in the RCIA, Cycle B.* Mahwah, N.J.: Paulist Press, 1987.

_____, editors. *Breaking Open the Word of God: Resources for Using the Lectionary for Catechesis in the RCIA, Cycle C.* Mahwah, N.J.: Paulist Press, 1988.

Share the Word. Washington, D.C.: Paulist National Catholic Evangelization Association, published bimonthly.

Shea, John. "Using Scripture in Pastoral Settings," *Chicago Studies*, Volume 23, 1984, pp. 131-139.

Sloyan, Gerard S. "Forming Catechumens Through the Lectionary," *Before and After Baptism: The Work of Teachers and Catechists*, James A. Wilde, editor. Chicago: Liturgy Training Publications, 1988.

Catholic Identity

Brophy, Don, and Edythe Westenhaver, editors. *The Story of Catholics in America.* Mawah, N.J.: Paulist Press, 1978.

Cogley, John. *Catholic America.* St. Louis, Mo.: Sheed and Ward, 1986.

Cunningham, Lawrence S. *The Catholic Heritage.* New York: Crossroad, 1985.

Delaney, John J. Editor. *Why Catholic?* Garden City, N.Y.: Image Books (Doubleday), 1980.

Dolan, Jay P. *The American Catholic Experience.* Notre Dame, Ind.: University of Notre Dame Press, 1992.

Dues, Greg. *Catholic Customs & Traditions: A Popular Guide.* Mystic, Conn.: Twenty-Third Publications, 1989.

Ellis, John Tracy. *American Catholicism.* Second Edition, Revised. Chicago: The University of Chicago Press, 1969.

Foley, Leonard, O.F.M, Editor. *Saint of the Day.* Revised Edition. Cincinnati: St. Anthony Messenger Press, 1990.

*Rohr, Richard, O.F.M., and Joseph Martos. *Why Be Catholic? Understanding Our Experience and Tradition.* Cincinnati: St. Anthony Messenger Press, 1989.

Church Documents

Book of Blessings (De Benedictionibus). International Commission on English in the Liturgy (ICEL). Collegeville, Minn.: The Liturgical Press, 1989.

Code of Canon Law (Codex Iuris Canonici). Latin-English Edition. Washington, D.C.: Canon Law Society of America, 1983.

Flannery, Austin P., editor. *Documents of Vatican II,* revised edition. Northport, N.Y.: Costello Publishing Co., 1988.

_____, editor. *Vatican II: More Postconciliar Documents,* revised edition. Northport, N.Y.: Costello Publishing Co., 1988.

Lectionary for Mass (Ordo lectionum missae). New York: Catholic Book Publishing Co., 1970.

Rite of Christian Initiation of Adults (Ordo initiationis christianae adultorum). International Commission on English in the Liturgy, Inc. (ICEL), and the Bishops' Committee on the Liturgy of the National Conference of Catholic Bishops. Chicago: Liturgy Training Publications, 1988.

Conversion

Duggan, Robert, editor. *Conversion and the Catechumenate.* Mahwah, N.J.: Paulist Press, 1984.

Griffin, Emilie. *Turning: Reflections on the Experience of Conversion.* New York: Doubleday, 1982.

Evangelization

Brennan, Patrick. *The Evangelizing Parish.* Allen, Texas: Tabor
Publications, 1987.

History

*Dujarier, Michel. *A History of the Catechumenate: The First Six
Centuries.* New York: William H. Sadlier, Inc., 1982.

*Field, Anne, O.S.B. *From Darkness to Light: What It Meant To
Become a Christian in the Early Church.* Ann Arbor, Mich.:
Servant Books, 1978.

Frend, W. H. C. *The Rise of Christianity.* Minneapolis: Augsburg
Fortress Publishers, 1984.

Happel, Stephen and David Tracy. *A Catholic Vision.* Philadelphia:
Fortress Press, 1984.

Stevenson, Kenneth W. *The First Rites: Worship in the Early Church.*
Collegeville, Minn.: The Liturgical Press, 1989.

Yarnold, Edward, S.J. *The Awe Inspiring Rites of Initiation:
Baptismal Homilies of the Fourth Century.* Slough, England: St.
Paul Publications, 1971.

Liturgy, Ritual, Sacraments

*Guzie, Tad. *The Book of Sacramental Basics.* Mahwah, N.J.: Paulist
Press, 1981.

Huck, Gabe. *Liturgy with Style and Grace.* Chicago: Liturgy Training
Publications, 1978.

*_____. *The Three Days: Parish Prayer in the Paschal Triduum.*
Revised Edition. Chicago: Liturgy Training Publications, 1992.

Kavanagh, Aidan, O.S.B. *On Liturgical Theology.* Collegeville,
Minn.: The Liturgical Press, 1984.

_____. *The Shape of Baptism: The Rite of Christian Initiation.*
Collegeville, Minn.: The Liturgical Press, 1978.

Kucharek, Casimir. *The Sacramental Mysteries: A Byzantine
Approach.* Allendale, N.J.: Alleluia Press, 1976.

Lopresti, James J. "Ritual and Conversion," *Christian Initiation Resources Reader*, Volume IV: *Mystagogia and Ministries*. New York: William H. Sadlier, Inc., 1984.

Martos, Joseph. *Doors to the Sacred: A Historical Introduction to Sacraments in the Catholic Church*. Expanded Edition. Tarrytown, N.Y.: Triumph Books, 1991.

Mitchell, Leonel L. *The Meaning of Ritual*. Ridgefield, Conn.: Morehouse Publishers, 1991.

Nocent, Adrian, O.S.B. *The Liturgical Year*. Four Volumes. Collegeville, Minn.: The Liturgical Press, 1977.

*Sourcebook for Sundays and Seasons. Chicago: Liturgy Training Publications, published annually.

*Tufano, Victoria M., editor. *Celebrating the Rites of Adult Initiation: Pastoral Reflections*. Chicago: Liturgy Training Publications, 1992.

Ministries

*Dunning, James B. *Ministries: Sharing God's Gifts*. Winona, Minn.: Saint Mary's Press, 1985.

Hart, Thomas N. *The Art of Christian Listening*. Mahwah, N.J.: Paulist Press, 1980.

*Lewinski, Ronald J. *Guide for Sponsors*. Revised Edition. Chicago: Liturgy Training Publications, 1987.

Power, David N. *Gifts that Differ: Lay Ministries Established and Unestablished*. New York: Pueblo Publishing Co., 1980.

Whitehead, James D., and Evelyn Eaton Whitehead. *Method in Ministry: Theological Reflection and Christian Ministry*. Minneapolis: The Seabury Press, 1980.

*Wilde, James A., editor. *A Catechumenate Needs Everybody*. Chicago: Liturgy Training Publications, 1988.

*_____, editor. *Before and After Baptism: The Work of Teachers and Catechists*. Chicago: Liturgy Training Publications, 1988.

*_____, editor. *Finding and Forming Sponsors and Godparents*. Chicago: Liturgy Training Publications, 1988.

_____, editor. *Parish Catechumenate: Pastors, Presiders, Preachers.*
Chicago: Liturgy Training Publications, 1988.

Mystagogy

Bruns, William R. *Cenacle Sessions: A Modern Mystagogy.* Mahwah,
N.J.: Paulist Press, 1991.

_____. *Easter Bread: Reflections on the Gospels of the Easter Season
for Neophytes and Their Companions.* Mahwah, N.J.: Paulist
Press, 1991.

Dunning, James B. "The Period of Mystagogia," *Christian Initiation
Resources Reader,* Volume IV: *Mystagogia and Ministries.*
New York: William H. Sadlier, Inc., 1984, pp. 7-18.

_____. "The Stages of Initiation: Part IV. The Sacraments of Initiation
and Afterwards," *Becoming a Catholic Christian.* New York:
William H. Sadlier, Inc., 1978, pp. 123-131.

Gusmer, Charles W. "Celebrating the Easter Season," *Christian
Initiation Resources Reader.* Volume IV: *Mystagogia and
Ministries.* New York: William H. Sadlier, Inc., 1984, pp.
31-39.

Mazza, Enrico. *Mystagogy: A Theology of Liturgy in the Patristic Age.*
Translated from the Italian by Matthew J. O'Connell.
Collegeville, Minn.: The Liturgical Press, 1989.

Organization

*Hinman, Karen. *How To Form a Catechumenate Team.* Chicago:
Liturgy Training Publications, 1986.

Prayer, Spirituality

Bloom, Anthony. *Beginning To Pray.* Mahwah, N.J.: Paulist Press,
1982.

Doherty, Barbara, S.P. *I Am What I Do: Contemplation and Human
Experience.* Chicago: The Thomas More Press, 1981.

_____. *Make Yourself an Ark.* Chicago: The Thomas More Press,
1984.

Green, Thomas H., S.J. *Weeds Among the Wheat*. Notre Dame, Ind.: Ave Maria Press, 1984.

Ignatius of Loyola. *The Spiritual Exercises*. Translated by Anthony Mottla. Garden City, N.Y.: Doubleday, 1964.

Kelsey, Morton T. *The Other Side of Silence: A Guide to Christian Meditation*. New York: Paulist Press, 1976.

Miller, William A. *Make Friends with Your Shadow: How To Accept and Use Positively the Negative Side of Your Personality*. Minneapolis: Augsburg Publishing House, 1981.

Nouwen, Henri J. M. *Reaching Out*. New York: Doubleday, 1975.

_____. *The Wounded Healer*. New York: Doubleday, 1979.

Powell, John, S.J. *He Touched Me: My Pilgrimage of Prayer*. Allen, Texas: Tabor Publishing, 1974.

Returning Catholics

Harmony, Sarah. *Re-membering: The Ministry of Welcoming Alienated Catholics*. Collegeville, Minn.: The Liturgical Press, 1991.

Scriptural Commentaries

Bergant, Dianne, C.S.A, and Robert J. Karris, O.F.M., general editors. *The Collegeville Bible Commentary*. Collegeville, Minn.: The Liturgical Press, 1989.

Brown, Raymond E., S.S., Joseph A. Fitzmyer, S.J., and Roland E. Murphy, O. Carm., editors. *The New Jerome Biblical Commentary*. Englewood Cliffs, N.J.: Prentice Hall, Inc., 1990.

*Senior, Donald, general editor. *The Catholic Study Bible*. New York: Oxford University Press, 1990.

Stuhlmueller, Carroll, C.P. *Biblical Meditations for Ordinary Time— Weeks 1-9*. Ramsey, N.J.: Paulist Press, 1984.

_____. *Biblical Meditations for Ordinary Time—Weeks 10-22*. Ramsey, N.J.: Paulist Press, 1984.

_____. *Biblical Meditations for Ordinary Time—Weeks 23-34*. Ramsey, N.J.: Paulist Press, 1984.

_____. *Biblical Meditations for Advent and the Christmas Season.* Ramsey, N.J.: Paulist Press, 1980.

_____. *Biblical Meditations for Lent.* Ramsey, N.J.: Paulist Press, 1978.

_____. *Biblical Meditations for the Easter Season.* Ramsey, N.J.: Paulist Press, 1980.

Spiritual Direction

Dyckman, Katherine and L. Patrick Carroll. *Inviting the Mystic, Supporting the Prophet: An Introduction to Spiritual Direction.* New York: Paulist Press, 1981.

Resources

Liturgy Training Publications
1800 North Hermitage Avenue
Chicago, IL 60622-1101
312-486-8970

North American Forum on the Catechumenate
5510 Columbia Pike, Suite 310
Arlington, VA 22204
703-671-0330

Publishing Services
United States Catholic Conference
3211 Fourth Street, NE
Washington, D.C. 20017
202-541-3090

Index